ARTHUR BOYD HOUGHTON

Sheik Hamil: A self-portrait. *c.*1870

Arthur Boyd Houghton

PAUL HOGARTH

GORDON FRASER

LONDON · 1981

First published in 1981 by
The Gordon Fraser Gallery Ltd, London and Bedford
Copyright © Paul Hogarth 1981

BRITISH LIBRARY CATALOGUING IN PUBLICATION DATA

Hogarth, Paul
  Arthur Boyd Houghton
  1. Houghton, Arthur Boyd
  760'.092'4   N6797.H68

  ISBN 0-900406-75-5

Unless otherwise stated, all dimensions are given in inches

Set in Monophoto Ehrhardt by Oliver Burridge & Co Ltd, Crawley, Sussex
and printed by Fletcher & Son, Ltd, Norwich
on Bewick Cartridge supplied by Frank Grunfeld Ltd
Bound by G & J Kitcat Ltd, London
Binding design engraved on vinyl by John Lawrence
Designed by Peter Guy

Contents

Introduction, 7

Acknowledgements, 9

I   Genial Pirate, 11

II   Susan, 23

III   Illustrator Extraordinary, 36

IV   The *Graphic*, 51

V   To America, 61

VI   Mother Ann's Commune, 75

VII   Going West, 86

VIII   The Buffalo Hunters, 100

IX   The Light That Failed, 113

X   Last Years, 123

Notes, 131

Appendix I: Select List of Works
   in Public Collections, 136

Appendix II: Select List of Publications
   containing Illustrations, 137

Select Bibliography, 139

Index, 141

Introduction

Painter, illustrator, caricaturist and Special Artist: in all these roles, Arthur Boyd Houghton was known during his short lifetime. Born at Kotagiri, a station in the Nilgiri Hills of Madras, India, in 1836, he was much the same age as du Maurier and Whistler; one of a generation deeply affected by the idealism of the Pre-Raphaelite Brotherhood. He died in 1875 and if remembered at all it is for the black and white illustrations made for Dalziel's *Arabian Nights* and magazines like *Good Words*, and for a handful of small genre paintings. Forgotten, as I will show, is his much more embracing achievement: he exhibited at major London galleries for over a decade and produced some hundred known paintings and over a thousand published drawings for books and periodicals.

As an artist, I am indebted to him for his way of seeing the world, and I should perhaps explain the nature of my debt. I first heard of Arthur Boyd Houghton in 1947. I was trying to direct my energies to observing the life of my own time and the always exacting art historian, Francis Klingender, urged me to study the illustrations of this little-known Victorian artist. I did not undertake this project until I chanced upon a set of dusty bound volumes of the early *Graphic*, to discover Houghton's 'Graphic America' and 'Paris Under the Commune'. Here was a master, an artist whose work was social without being didactic.

As my own work as an illustrator took me to America during the sixties, I again studied 'Graphic America' (Houghton also wrote the accompanying articles) and came to realize that the writing contained many hidden clues to his personality. I expressed some thoughts on this subject in an essay published in *The American West* (V, 6, November, 1968). This was followed by an extended version, again on his Western travels, as a chapter of my book about Victorian artist-travellers in America, *Artists on Horseback* (1972). 'Graphic America' and

Houghton's other ventures into the wider world of his time led me to attempt a more rounded study of his life and work taking into account his work as a painter, as well as his woodblock illustrations buried deep in a mountain of long-forgotten books and periodicals.

The task of gathering all this material together has been both exhilarating and frustrating; exhilarating because it has enabled me to delve deeply into the world of Victorian art and journalism to discover much that has been inaccessible; frustrating because so much of Houghton's work could not be traced.

Houghton was, in so many ways, one of the most contemporary artists of his time, yet it is only in retrospect that the peculiar haunting quality of his art has been realized and appreciated. Bourgeois realist he was, but during his short lifetime he was dismissed as an 'eccentric', and received but limited recognition. Although his work now seems to be closely related in style to that of Holman Hunt, Winslow Homer and du Maurier, his work was, and still is, difficult to fit into a particular school. Indeed, his paintings and illustrations were thought so contrary to current taste that time and time again he was accused of flaunting his non-conformity. There are only six studies of his work worth mentioning (see Bibliography), and only one of these, Laurence Housman's *Arthur Boyd Houghton* (1896), has the distinction of having been published as a book. None of them provides a biography which takes all his achievements into account.

A certain amount of interest was shown in Houghton's work as a result of the first public exhibitions of Victorian illustration in 1901 and 1917, which the pioneer collector of Victorian illustration, Harold T. Hartley, had organized at the Victoria & Albert Museum and the Royal Academy of Arts. These important exhibitions led to further studies, and a follower of Houghton, the illus-

Arthur Boyd Houghton, by George du Maurier.
From *Punch*, October 24, 1868.

trator, E. J. Sullivan (1869–1933) was moved to devote a chapter of his *Art of Illustration* (1921) to comparing Houghton with Frederick Sandys (1829–1904), another adherent of the Pre-Raphaelite movement who worked as an illustrator. Sullivan had published what he had been able to discover, but like Housman he found that the family had 'little record, scarcely anything in the way of papers'. Sullivan concluded that such a family, accustomed to travelling light, had destroyed such papers as were not of immediate concern. 'To such', he wrote, 'the past is done with; so that unfortunately there is no less documented life that that of Boyd Houghton'.

I have tried assiduously to unearth more facts. At times during my researches I felt as if there were a conspiracy to destroy all trace of Houghton. Firstly, it took

not a little time to discover his descendants. Here, I owe a great debt of gratitude to the Archives Department of the Tate Gallery, who made available the last known address of Houghton's grandson, Mr Sydney Davis. The address was more than forty years out of date and it was not until 1972, with the assistance of Ruth Boswell, that I finally succeeded in tracking Mr Davis down. I then learnt that as recently as 1971 a collection of the artist's papers had been inadvertently destroyed by a distraught member of the family anxious to clear her attic of accumulated, and as she thought, useless family rubbish!

Mr Davis was able to add a little more to Sullivan, but even then the 'conspiracy' persisted. Certain birth certificates could not be located in the General Register Office at Somerset House; houses in which the artist and his family had lived in Kentish Town and Hampstead were demolished – one on the very day I went to look at it! From his grave in Paddington Cemetery, a handsome black marble cross had been removed and broken up with sledgehammers; no living member of the family even knew he had been buried there.

Added to this was the baffling lack of adequate reference to him in the reminiscences and autobiographies of friends and acquaintances, even though he was frequently acknowledged by them as one of the most gifted artists of his day. Some of his more intimate friends died young; one, the once celebrated, now forgotten publisher, Alexander Strahan, did not live to complete his autobiography. Last, but certainly not least, is the mysterious disappearance of almost all of Houghton's later oriental-cum-biblical pictures.

Despite the 'conspiracy', many new facts have been discovered. Perhaps the most valuable was that of a group of paintings long thought to have been lost. Also, thanks to the indefatigable Ian Baxter of India Office Records, much has now come to light of the Houghton family background.

Yet my book is not so much about who Houghton was as an individual, but essentially what he was. It is not an attempt to see him from the outside, but to see the world with his eyes. He was a unique commentator on the social life of his period and, Victorian as some of his scenes of contemporary life may appear to us today, he helped to shape the approach which has led to the pictorial social comment of our own time. He was a man of the world as well as an artist, a realist as well as an idealist, and during his short life he chose to confront the changing values of the time without losing the essential integrity of his vision. Yet his background was woven closely into the fabric of his art, and his work and life bound together so intimately that they must be considered as a whole. To understand him, to appreciate fully his art, we must know the people he knew, the places he visited, and the circumstances that shaped his life.

Acknowledgements

I should like to express my appreciation to the many who have given generous assistance in my quest for material. I am especially indebted to Houghton's grandson (son of Georgina Maud, the artist's eldest daughter), Sydney Charles Houghton Davis of Guildford, Surrey, for supplying documents, letters, photographs, and personal reminiscences; for allowing me to view paintings by Houghton in his possession, and those owned by members of the family whom he approached on my behalf. To Jack Ironside Wood of Chelmsford, Essex (son of Cecily, the artist's youngest daughter) for further information about the family. To the late Winifred Poingdestre of Hurstpierpoint, Sussex, the artist's grandniece, for permitting me to view her collection of works by Houghton and his eldest brother, William; and for valuable assistance in helping me trace further works. To Colin Davis of Rapallo, Italy, Houghton's great-grandson, for permission to reproduce *Sheik Hamil*. To John Webb, for his photographs of many of the paintings. To Eric de Maré, for the loan of much valuable illustrative material.

I also owe a debt of gratitude to the following archivists, curators, collectors, librarians and interested individuals: Sir Colin Anderson; Mrs Louise Ambler; Julia Blackburn; Mary Bennett; Anthony Burton; James Claydon; Prof. W. E. Fredeman; Richard Green; Julian Hartnoll; Dr James Harle; Mrs Ruth Harris; the late Sir Harold Hartley; Sidney C. Hutchison; Sinclair Hamilton; Richard Hathaway; Elizabeth Johnson; Susan Lambert; Allan R. Life; the late David McKibborn of the Boston Athenaeum; Jeremy Maas; Douglas Mathews; Keith Melder; Bernard Myers; J. L. Naimester; A. McIntosh Patrick; the late Henry C. Pitz; Mrs Phoebe Peebles; Derek Pepys-Whiteley; Graham Reynolds; Paul D. Riley; Stephanie Loeb Stepanek; Dinah Southern; Mrs Virginia Surtees; Sotheby's of Bond Street & Belgravia; Christopher Wood.

All the pictures in this book are reproduced by permission of their owners or, in the case of those in public collections, of the trustees of the museum or gallery.

Illustration for 'Homeward Bound', a poem by William Allingham, 1866. Wood engraving. From *A Round of Days*. Print Room, British Museum, London. Houghton used members of his family as well as family reminiscences in many of his illustrations. Although himself a baby at the time, he imagines the return of his father and himself as a boy from India, greeted at the docks by his mother.

I: Genial Pirate

Arthur Boyd Houghton was a rare type of artist. The jewel-like intensity of his vision, whether depicting a London street scene or a subject from his own family life, has a haunting immediacy which transcends time. In the finest of his earlier woodblock illustrations and paintings he created an extraordinary universe of rosy-cheeked children, of long-haired beautiful women, of impulsive youth and venerable old age, in settings so various and idyllic as to make it all a never-never land, threatened by the reality of the outside world.

The death of his young wife Susan in 1864 after only three years of marriage almost demoralized him. From that moment his world began to break up, for the role of the family in his life's work had meant everything to him. For a while his travels to America and France diverted some of his acute sense of loss, but by 1872 he had turned to embrace, as Sullivan tells us, 'a feverish life of such excitement as the Bohemia of the day provided'. Three years later, at the age of 39, he was dead.

Before he ever met Susan he had begun to report the contemporary world as he saw it, nakedly and honestly. After her death this main characteristic of his art and spirit reasserted itself all the more strongly. What was remarkable was that he exposed the failings of humanity without unduly mocking them, although his humour was often mordant and searching. He was the natural heir to the finest social satirists of the seventeenth and eighteenth centuries, Callot and Hogarth. One also sees other influences: the early Millais and Brown, and even Hunt, Utamaro and Menzel. But Callot prevails in the shadowy irony of his line. Van Gogh immediately recognized the influence: 'He had', he wrote to Theo, 'something mysterious like Goya, with a wonderful soberness which reminds me of Meryon'.

His was an age in which middle-class life had for the first time come freely and undisputably to the forefront, and he was, like Keene, its interpreter. But in Houghton there are undertones of unrest, and unlike Keene he realized that influences were developing that would make the world much less comfortable for the middle-class generations of the future.

Both his parents came from upper-class English stock.[1] His mother, the strong-minded Sophia Elizabeth Renshaw, came from a well-to-do Anglo-Indian family, the daughter of the Customs Master of Bombay. The man she married, the equally independent John Michael Houghton, was the son of a naval surgeon on the East Indiaman, *Britannia*. He had been given a sound classical education and left England at 14 as a midshipman on the East Indiaman, *Elphinstone*, on her voyage to China in 1812. Shortly after reaching Canton, he transferred to the Hydrographic Service of the East India Company's Marine and eventually became a draughtsman with the rank of Lieutenant. By the time of his marriage in 1823 Michael Houghton held the rank of Captain or Commander, and was a highly respected official stationed at Bombay.

The marriage appears to have been solidly Victorian. There were nine children all close to each in age, five sons and four daughters. Arthur was the most talented and unusual and also the closest to his father, whose adventurous spirit he inherited. When Arthur was a year old the family returned to England. His father, suffering from ill-health, was given three years' furlough. However, he decided to remain with his large and still-growing family rather than endure a solitary life in India, leaving his wife to supervise their education – which was then the custom.

Like most Anglo-Indian families, the Houghtons seldom remained in one place very long. In this they were a typical product of the Victorian Empire. They had lost their roots in the old country and the sense of

The artist's father, John Michael Houghton, by Arthur Boyd Houghton, c.1868.
Oil on canvas. 25 × 19. Davis collection, Guildford.

unity was maintained by the family group rather than by one fixed residence or place being thought of as home.[2]

The constantly shifting surroundings of Arthur's childhood had an effect of the greatest importance upon both his temperament and his development as an artist. One of his earliest newspaper illustrations, *Uncle John with the Young Folks*, which appeared as a full-page wood engraving in the Christmas number of the *Illustrated London News* (December 23, 1865: p. 618), depicts his white-haired father, presiding over an enormous children's party on a truly Anglo-Indian scale. Houghton's innate gregariousness is strikingly revealed. Such events, an important part of the family's well-organized mobility, obviously helped him to fit in with many disparate groups of people, and to respond to them in his art, not only as a witness but also as a participant.

India especially made its presence felt in the curios and costumes that accompanied the family wherever they lived, and which constantly appeared in his paintings and illustrations. It is easy to guess the effect of both his parents' recollections and those of his brothers, particularly his oldest brother William, upon his impressionable imagination.[3] Houghton heard described the teeming vitality of Indian life, the variety of characters and costumes, the young army or navy officers resplendent with creepers and exotic blossoms, all set against the fantastic pinnacles and awesome gorges of the Western Ghats of the Bombay Presidency. From such tales of the East, he derived imaginative stimulus. The extraordinary ensembles of Eastern types and the mountain landscapes in his illustrations for the Dalziel edition of the *Arabian Nights* were recreated out of the vividness of such family reminiscences and pictorial records.

He loved to draw and did so from an early age. While his mother insisted that he should have a respectable career, his father, wishing him to become a surgeon, concealed his disapproval of such artistic leanings and showed him his own sketchbooks of ships, harbours and coastlines made to illustrate his maps of the East India Company's Surveys of the China Sea and the Gulf of Persia.

On leaving school at sixteen Arthur was enrolled at a London medical school, but the family's hopes that he would pursue a surgeon's career were short-lived. He

Susan Elizabeth Gronow, the
artist's future wife, *c*.1860.
Oil on canvas. 13 × 10½.
Harris collection, Oxford.

biography said that Leigh – wearing a skull-cap and black velvet smock – would 'stride about among easels and antique statues gesticulating wildly, rolling out sarcasm and invective in very choice Italian'.

A strongly-built man then in his forties, Leigh kept order by means of a savagely biting wit which earned him the nickname of 'Dagger'. He ran his studio after the style of the French master Gleyre and, like Gleyre's celebrated atelier, Leigh's swarmed with a motley company of bewhiskered, would-be artists wearing sombreros and cloaks in the Paris fashion of La Bohème. He was a devoted teacher, whose pupils attended his classes long after they had succeeded in entering the Royal Academy Schools. Under Leigh, Houghton not only learned to draw and handle paint, but to discuss ideas and acquire a ready wit of his own.[5]

In 1854 he entered the Antique school of the Royal Academy Schools as a fully-fledged art student. He may have survived two, perhaps three years, and probably passed into the Life school, but it is unlikely that he stayed long enough to enter the Painting school. His reasons for not doing so are easy to guess. The arts were attracting greater numbers of young men of education and social position, and with the decline of the old system of studio apprenticeship to a master, the Royal Academy Schools were grossly overcrowded.

Under such conditions, Leigh's and particularly the Artists' Society became unofficial centres of postgraduate studies. The Artists' Society,[6] or as it was commonly called, 'The Langham', especially offered facilities not generally available at this time. These included nude and undraped models, lectures and conversations, a library and a lending wardrobe of historical costumes.

Here, cheek by jowl with older artists like Keene and Tenniel, students learned to run the race against time with a set weekly subject for illustration, written up in chalk on a large slate on the previous Friday. During the week all had time to ponder the given themes, what to select and how to treat it. Thus prepared, they were expected to complete a design, either on canvas in oil, or on paper in watercolour, in two hours. Such sessions often took on a dramatic atmosphere as each member, 'urged by a spirit of honourable rivalry', attempted to complete his work.

attended medical school for two years and, having secured his father's approval, lost no time in applying himself to more congenial studies at the evening classes of Leigh's General Practical School of Art at 79 Newman Street, Soho. It was romantically ideal for his purpose. Newman Street, in the north of Soho, was the centre of what was then the established artists' quarter of mid-Victorian England. Leigh's prepared candidates for admission to the prestigious Royal Academy Schools. But the atmosphere was informal. He could come and go as he pleased; the place was open from six in the morning until ten at night. The curriculum consisted mainly of life-drawing, drawing from the antique, and perspective, in which the master himself joined his pupils in improvised illustrations of art, literature and politics.

James Mathew Leigh was a cousin of the celebrated music-hall comedian Charles Mathews and no mean performer himself.[4] A dull evening might be enlivened by a spontaneous impersonation, his favourite being the Italian patriot Mazzini, then in exile in London. An early acquaintance of Houghton's, the painter Henry Stacy Marks, also attended Leigh's, and in his auto-

Toby Belch, Viola and Aguecheek
A scene from Shakespeare's
*Twelfth Night. c.*1854.
Oil on wood panel. 16 × 12.
Folger Shakespeare Library,
Washington, D.C.

The 'Langham', as one member, J. G. Marks, said, 'stood in something like the same relation to Leigh's that the Universities do to the Schools, and study there formed a regular part of the curriculum of many of Leigh's old students'. In this fraternal atmosphere Houghton began not only to paint pictures, but to increase his capacity to evolve images in relation to specific themes.

Leigh taught that the highest form of art was history painting. He took themes from the ever-popular Shakespeare and contemporary historical novelists such as Scott and Bulwer Lytton, and encouraged his pupils to

interest themselves in serious drama. Accordingly, Houghton's earliest works comprised a series of small oils, illustrating scenes from contemporary performances of Shakespeare and Goldsmith. These leave much to be desired, but the very range of subjects reflect his eager enthusiasm. All show a medley of influences, especially from Frith, Horsley and Ward, the currently popular exponents of historical genre. But towards the end of the fifties Houghton was absorbing other influences, some received while tramping the streets at all hours. He showed a fascinated interest in London life and made sketches of street scenes with a view to producing more

The Deserter 1859.
Oil on canvas.
10 × 14⅛.
Iveagh Bequest,
Kenwood House, London.
(above)

Punch and Judy c.1860.
Oil on canvas.
14 × 10.
The Tate Gallery, London.
(right)

Volunteers Marching Out, 1860.
Oil on canvas.
10 × 13¾.
Iveagh Bequest,
Kenwood House, London.
(facing page, above)

Volunteers 1861.
Oil on canvas.
12 × 15½.
The Tate Gallery, London.
(facing page, below)

ambitious paintings of modern subjects.

London of the fifties was a spectacle no artist could easily ignore. Huge, with a population of over two and a half million, and sprawling like an octopus, it was a city unlike any other. Every day, as Houghton made his way from his parents' house in peacefully suburban St John's Wood, he encountered such extremes of glitter and squalor, the high life juxtaposed against the low, that he must have felt he was entering another world. Certainly, the area to the north of Oxford Street (between Regent Street and Tottenham Court Road) in the affluent West End where Leigh's and the Langham were located, had its share of such contrasts. All *seemed* respectable enough until one looked beneath the surface. Oxford Street itself was crowded with brightly-coloured horse-buses; hansom-cabs and saddle-horses passed by with now and then a more splendid carriage, with a coachman perched on top and footmen behind. Like the Strand, it was a dividing line between rich and poor. Behind the famous street, as inquisitive observers like Hippolyte Taine discovered, were 'stifling alleys thick with human effluvia (and) pale children crouching on filthy staircases'.

Houghton had only to walk a half-mile westward to encounter the outlying reaches of the 'Holy Land'; a vast congested labyrinth of back streets, yards and passages 'crammed with desperate outcast humanity', living their lives literally on the streets. Here indeed was where the tide of life, in Dr Johnson's words, was fullest. People quarrelled, shouted and fought with one another against a continuous clatter of coal-carts, brewer's drays, milk-trucks and baker's barrows, to mention some of the more orthodox trades.

For lighter entertainment, Chesney informs us in his *The Victorian Underworld*, there were the ballad singers, holding forth at the doors of the gin-palaces while young bloods inside slaked their thirst with 'blue ruin'. The bell of a crier was heard in the distance, and pan-pipes and the beating drum of a Punch-and-Judy show sounded in a nearby alley, where a thickening throng of urchins and errand boys foregathered to watch. As afternoon became evening, the lamplighter appeared, threading his way through, pausing here and there to illuminate the gathering darkness.

Houghton saw it all like a legacy bequeathed to him

by Hogarth, which indeed it was. And he proceeded to create from such first-hand observations a series of paintings full of incident and more diverse than anything he had attempted before. One such picture was *Recruiting Party* (Iveagh Bequest, Kenwood), suggested by the recruiting of susceptible youths for the Army: a common sight in the slums of Victorian London. It was sent to the Portland Gallery for the Twelfth Annual Exhibition of the National Institution of Fine Arts in 1859, and was well received. Thornbury, an old friend from Leigh's, now art critic of the influential *Athenaeum* (March 26, 1859; p. 426) rose to the occasion and praised 'its Hogarthian fullness and variety'.

Houghton did not exhibit again at the Portland Gallery until 1861 when he sent *Poor Nomads* (Iveagh Bequest, Kenwood). The impression this created showed how important his work was becoming in the opinion of his contemporaries. Marks, writing as 'Drypoint' in *The Spectator* (March 16, 1861: p. 277) commented favourably on its 'great feeling for character'. In *Poor Nomads*, Hogarth is a strong influence. A family of wandering entertainers is surrounded by a London crowd of all ages, characters and occupations. Two mutes stand at a door, and a child performer begs from one. The street urchins, a drunkard, swells passing by and volunteer riflemen were, added Marks, 'all good, showing great discrimination and fidelity of expression'.

Houghton continued painting such scenes of London life, and in 1860 came up with the delightful *Punch and Judy* (Tate Gallery). But it is with *Volunteers* (Tate Gallery), *Volunteers Marching Out* (Iveagh Bequest, Kenwood), and *Holborn in 1861* (Anderson Collection), that he made his major contribution to modern genre painting. All are contemporary subjects; the first two sparked off by the Volunteer movement which swept Britain during 1859-60, while *Holborn in 1861* is a manifestation of his enthusiasm for the Pre-Raphaelites, most of all, Ford Madox Brown. In *The Volunteers* and *Volunteers Marching Out*, one is made very aware that this was a middle-class game which neatly combined physical exercise and congenial company with a satisfying if complacent feeling of performing a patriotic duty. In *Holborn in 1861*, his delight in the minutiae of character traits makes the painting a haunting chronicle of Victorian

society, telling in the complexity of its symbolism.

It is likely that Houghton first saw the work of his real master, Brown, if not at the Pre-Raphaelite Exhibition at Russell Place, 1857, then certainly later at the semi-private exhibitions of the Hogarth Club from 1858 to '61 (his friend Thomas Morten joined in 1858). Its founders included the Pre-Raphaelites Brown and Morris, as well as William Michael Rossetti, critic and brother of Dante Gabriel. The Hogarth Club, named after the master who so largely concerned himself with the everyday life of his times, sought to discuss ways and means by which a democratic art might flourish in what was an undemo-

cratic society. To this end, meetings were held with previews of members' works destined for exhibition at the Royal Academy, the British Institution, and other annual or bi-annual shows in Birmingham, Liverpool, and Manchester.

At mid-century, the most creative figures in English art were the Pre-Raphaelites, Millais, Hunt, Rossetti and Brown. Since 1848, their rebellion against the Academy had periodically enlivened the Victorian art world. What they were rebelling against was listed by Hunt himself as: 'monkeyana ideas, Books of Beauty and Choirester Boys'. But their attempts to replace such well-worn subjects with those which had genuine content, vividly portrayed and passionately experienced, brought abuse and adverse criticism upon their heads. It took Ruskin's celebrated letter to *The Times* during 1851 to redress the balance.

Principles are inclined to have a short life, limited to the early enthusiasms of a young artist. By the mid-1850s the original impulse of Pre-Raphaelitism showed signs of slackening. Millais, the great talent of the movement, had embraced the Royal Academy and was on his way to becoming the most successful portrait painter of the century. Rossetti, under the influence of chloral, was as Ruskin put it, 'half lost in medievalism and Dante'. Hunt had become an eccentric mannerist. Only Ford Madox Brown continued to develop the principles of Pre-Raphaelitism whilst relating them closely to modern life. His two great pictures, *The Last of England* (1852–5) (Art Gallery and Museum, Birmingham), and *Work* (1852–65) (City Art Gallery, Manchester), invite favourable comparison with his French contemporary Courbet, although Brown's realism, as Gere reminds us ('always uncompromising, sometimes grotesque, often satirical'), was of course in the direct tradition of the modern morality picture. In painting such scenes, which revealed his Christian Socialist sympathies as well as an involvement with the life of his time, Brown was pointing a way which Houghton and a whole new school of genre artists would follow.

Although realism as championed by Brown was very much in tune with the materialism of the English middle classes, it gained but little acceptance. Brown, as Klingender pointed out, 'expressed experiences that went to the roots of English life'. Such paintings as *The Last of England* and *Work* depicted everyday events such as emigration and the process of labour with a poetically true realism. But his pictures remained unsold for years, and after disputes with the Royal Academy, Brown became an implacable hater of the art establishment. He ceased to exhibit at the Academy after 1853, preferring to show his work at the Hogarth Club, or the annual exhibitions of the Birmingham Society of Artists, the Liverpool Academy and the Manchester Royal Institution; he eventually acquired some patronage from more enlightened merchants and stockbrokers.

The Oyster Stall 1872. Pen and wash. $4\frac{5}{8} \times 6\frac{7}{8}$. Museum of Fine Arts, Boston, Massachusetts. The influence of Houghton's early explorations into the street life of London can be seen in this original drawing for *Judy*.

The objection to Brown was, of course, as much social and political as it was aesthetic. Persuaded by the idealism of early Victorian socialism, he sided with those who saw the workers as proud heroic figures. The rest of the population made capital out of their labour. It was the four navvies, digging a pit in a London suburban street, who were the *real* pillars of society. What made Brown superior to other painters in Houghton's view was not that he transformed reality into something hauntingly significant, but that he also saw reality more intensely. *Holborn in 1861*, although not without a whole series of lessons in Christian morality and social comment, reveals Houghton as a much less didactic observer than Brown, with a sense of humour much closer to English life.

As his work began to gain in originality, Houghton increased his efforts to dispose of his pictures by sending them to other major London exhibitions. By 1861 he was a frequent exhibitor at the British Institution and the Royal Academy as well as the Portland Gallery. He followed the example of Brown and the Pre-Raphaelites and even sent works to the Liverpool Academy and Manchester Royal Institution. But he was no more successful than Brown. That his paintings remained unsold

A Conjugal Difficulty 1860.
Oil on canvas.
10 × 8.
Private collection, Oxford.
Houghton was anxious to marry
Susan but he had little other
than determination to prove
himself. In this early genre
scene, the subject appears to
be a lover's quarrel under the
jetty at Broadstairs.

underlines the bourgeois criteria that guided the average buyer's taste around the middle of the nineteenth century. He generally wished to be told a story, to be entertained, and to receive a little moral instruction. But he usually believed that the art that best satisfied these demands had to rely on the imagery of cosy interiors, of pastoral country life, or the remote past. It did not deal with the life of the cities, nor with social problems; it did not make any demands, but instead encouraged the most maudlin sentimentality.

All this posed a challenge to Houghton's adventurous spirit. The direction his style would follow was now established, along with his inability (combined with a stubborn unwillingness) to compromise with the de-

mands of the general art-buying public. So, despite some encouraging reactions to the pictures he exhibited at the Portland Gallery and the admiration of his friends and fellow-members of the 'Langham', Houghton had misgivings about his prospects.[7] 'Long before a student can hope to be recognized', wrote the critic of the *Art Journal* (1864: p. 150), 'he must not only be a picture-maker but a breadwinner'. Faced by this daunting prospect and his migraine headaches, he must have felt as unfit to practise as an artist as he had previously felt about taking up the surgeon's trade. But then he fell in love, and that profound emotional experience gave him a new release of energy and determination.

'Courtship' 1865. Wood engraving. Vignette for poem, 'A Life in A Year' by Dora Greenwell. From *A Round of Days*. The British Library, London.

Susan c.1861. Oil on canvas
$9\frac{1}{2} \times 7\frac{1}{2}$. Known as *Lady with
a Book*. The Tate Gallery,
London.

II: Susan

Susan Elizabeth Gronow's attraction for Houghton was both physical and spiritual. His pictures show how profoundly her beauty moved him, and in her large brown eyes, smoothly olive complexion, and above all in her lustrous dark brown hair, lay Susan's appeal to his sense of beauty. It is possible that they first became acquainted as the result of Captain Houghton's sociable habit of making himself known to congenial neighbours. The Gronows, an old and wealthy family, had an estate at Ash Hall, Glamorganshire, in Wales, and maintained a substantial London residence at 21 Carlton Hill; this was the street next to Clifton Road East, where the Houghtons lived at this time. Houghton may have become acquainted with Susan through his young sister, Grace; both girls are shown talking to Marks in *Volunteers*, which predates the marriage.

Susan, some five years younger than Houghton, is an elusive figure who left nothing behind but her haunting presence in numerous paintings and illustrations, immortalized by Houghton's passionate devotion. She was as vital to him as Elizabeth Siddal was to Dante Gabriel Rossetti.

The Gronows, although conventional, were not altogether lacking in cultural awareness. Nevertheless, they were guardedly suspicious of those who actually hoped to *live* by the arts. Mrs Gronow looked on Houghton with little approval. So little indeed that she was reported to have placed a curse upon Susan on her deathbed. Mr Gronow (chaplain to the Fourth Earl of Lisburne and a younger brother of the Regency blade, Captain Howell Rees Gronow) was more philosophical and appreciated Houghton for his obvious qualities, regardless of his less affluent background. The couple's love for each other exceeded the bounds of the discretion that appeared to be necessary; Susan became pregnant and they were married with family compliance (the ceremony was witnessed by Thomas Gronow and Grace Houghton), at St Mary's, the parish church of St Marylebone, on February 26, 1861.

Marriage to Susan gave Houghton the security and motivation he so desperately needed. He moved from his parents' home in St John's Wood to Richmond, where he took a three-year lease of a Georgian cottage house at 4 Adelaide Villas, St Mary's Grove. Here, later that year, on October 12, their first child, Arthur Herbert, was born. Susan became his favourite model, and he began to produce a continuing series of small, exquisite scenes of family life with Susan as their perfect period centrepiece. The essence of true domestic contentment, they seem like a thanksgiving for his newly-found regeneration. In true Pre-Raphaelite fashion, his family and closest friends served as models for him to assert the virtues of family life as an article of faith in himself, and consequently in people generally.

Houghton's image of his family provided the cohesiveness essential for his art to develop more fully. No less important than the inexhaustible source of models in relaxed and everyday postures were the succeeding family experiences which introduced a whole new range of subject matter. For Houghton, the bourgeois realist, ordinary situations and the events of everyday life were as worthy of portrayal as the themes of High Art, the heroes of antiquity or Christian saints. And increasingly he placed a positive value on the prosperous sectors of modern life as well as the low, the humble, and the socially outcast. In doing so, he met the demand for contemporaneity, so much the essence of mid-nineteenth century realism.

He began with a memorable small canvas, entitled *Lady with a Book* (Tate Gallery), which could simply be described as a lover's tribute to Susan and her gently bewitching beauty; it was never exhibited, and like a

The Family 1861. Oil on canvas. $17\frac{1}{2} \times 11\frac{1}{2}$. Sir Colin Anderson collection, London.

The Donkey Ride 1862. Oil on canvas. 10×12. Fogg Art Museum, Cambridge, Ma

Renaissance miniature, accompanied the artist on his travels. A second larger canvas, entitled *Baby*, or as the artist called it, *The Family* (Anderson Collection), achieves the highest point in the development of both his style and technique at this time. In this superb picture is contained the very essence of mid-Victorian domesticity; the genteel upper middle-class English family. It represents Susan, stunningly beautiful in a puce-coloured crinoline day dress, playing with her infant son on her lap. Grace looks on, sharing Susan's delight, while in the background, glancing up from *The Times* with ill-disguised pride, is white-haired Captain Michael Houghton.

Not all of Houghton's scenes of family life were devoted to Susan and the children. The seaside offered him an alternative setting, and here he occasionally extended the circle to include his brothers and sisters and their children. Ignored by previous generations as a source of pleasure, a seaside excursion became, with the advent of a comfortable railway journey, even more popular than the traditional country walk. Spring, summer and autumn were times of great excitement for the young family as the artist whisked Susan, Arthur and later

[24]

Ramsgate Sands 1863. Oil on canvas. 9½ × 11¾. Also known as *Out of Doors*. The Tate Gallery, London. The seaside
as a source of pleasure and relaxation, rather than a background for the hazardous activities of sailors and fishermen,
was still a fairly recent phenomenon at this time. Just as recent was the notion to paint it outdoors, as the artist's
original title suggests.

Georgina (their second child, born in 1862) off for a few days at Margate, Brighton or Broadstairs. But Houghton's favourite place was Ramsgate, an old seaport with fine yellow sands, made famous by William Powell Frith's canvas *Life at the Seaside* (Ramsgate Sands). Compared with Frith's vast social narrative, however, Houghton's *Ramsgate Sands* (Tate Gallery) seems like a page from an autograph album.

The spell of Susan's gentle femininity reached beyond his painting, providing him with never-ending inspiration for the woodblock drawings which he was now producing in increasing numbers for the Dalziels (see

'The artist with his wife and son'. Engraved by the Brothers Dalziel. From *Good Words*, 1862. Print Room, The British Museum, London.

Susan with Arthur, playing '*Coach and Horses*'. Illustration for 'My Treasure', a poem by 'R.M.' Engraved by the Brothers Dalziel. From *Good Words*, 1862. Print Room, Victoria & Albert Museum, London. The illustration provided a point of departure for at least two known paintings, including that on the facing page.

Coach and Horses 1864. Oil on canvas. $9\frac{1}{2} \times 11\frac{1}{2}$. Davis collection, Guildford.

Chapter III). Under her persuasive influence he began creating some of his finest illustrations. And it was with this series of idyllic genre scenes, done during the first two years of his marriage, that he made his really noteworthy appearance as an illustrator. These appeared in *Good Words*, a popular monthly, and began with a full-page woodblock entitled *Coach and Horses* (3, 1862:

p. 504), for the verse 'My Treasure' by 'R.M.'. The infant Arthur is depicted holding the reins of Susan's long tresses.

Almost monthly, others followed, including an illustration for 'True or False', a verse by Queen Victoria's favourite poet Adelaide Ann Proctor (3, 1862: p. 721), a self-portrait with Susan holding the infant Arthur

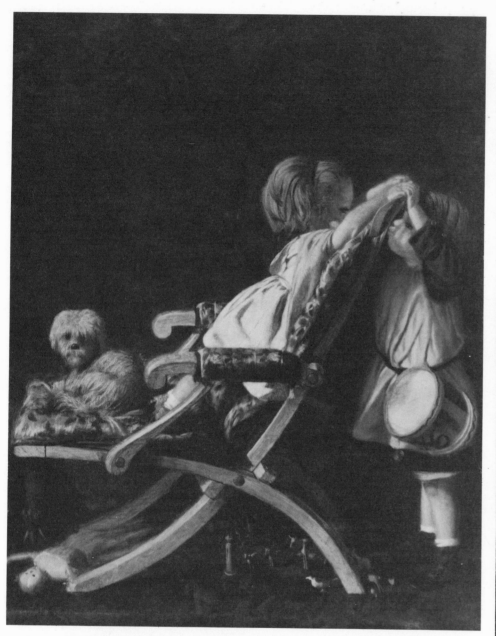

Interior with Children at Play c.1866. Oil on canvas. 9¾ × 8. Also known as *Playmates*. Ashmolean Museum, Oxford. Another example of the artist's habit of painting oil versions of woodblock illustrations which he either liked himself, or which had occasioned favourable comment from the Dalziels.

Kiss Me. An illustration for the poem 'Childhood'. Engraved by the Brothers Dalziel. From *Good Words*, 1863. Print Room, Victoria & Albert Museum, London.

above his head for the baby's toes to be affectionately squeezed, and *Kiss Me* (4, 1863: p. 636) for another unsigned verse, 'Childhood', which depicts Arthur and Georgina playing. All these illustrations are superbly drawn evocations of the warmth and intimacy of his family life, heightened by the fragile, almost doll-like beauty of Susan and the poignant innocence of his young children. But like the hero in a mid-Victorian novel, Houghton's happiness was to be of short duration and his idyllic family life was shortly to become nothing more than a painful memory. A third child, a daughter Cecily, was born June 12, 1864, and then, four weeks later, on July 13, Susan died of pyaemia, or blood poisoning.[1]

Overwrought by the unbelievable loss, he fell into a mood of deep self-reproach, blaming himself for Susan's death, although in the sixties childbearing was a hazardous business. All too frequently blood poisoning followed childbirth owing to the almost total absence of medical hygiene. Houghton fled for solace to his parents and subsequently they decided to move back from Margate where they had retired. He moved to a larger house in Hampstead.[2] Here his father, now a stricken old man, kept to his chair, while his mother, a genial matriarch, exercised what control she could over her unfortunate son and his three lively children.

As if to reasure himself that something of Susan could never be lost, Houghton continued painting his children, making his venerable devoted old father the centre of the family group. One notable example, *Mending the Jack-in-the-Box* (Davis Collection) was shown at the Royal Academy of 1866. Another painting, *The Artist's Father with Cecily* (Poingdestre Collection), also dates from this year, as does the familiar *Interior with Children Playing*, or as the artist called it, *Playmates* (Ashmolean Museum, Oxford). But no matter how he tried, the image of his family could never again be a source of inspiration to him.

For a time Houghton turned to modern life subjects to seek the meaning or expression of his essentially realist values of truth and sincerity. Significantly, he found it only in the most ordinary of people, the last to consider themselves heroes. But at least the anonymity of the larger outside world helped him absorb and ease the painful memories.

[29]

Mending the Jack-in-the-Box c.1865–6. Oil on canvas. 30 × 25. Davis collection, Guildford.

The Jewel Box c.1868.
Watercolour. $7 \times 4\frac{5}{8}$.
Hartley Collection, Museum
of Fine Arts, Boston. The
artist's younger daughter,
Cecily, examining the contents
of a jewel box at the house in
King Henry's Road. Through
the window can be seen the
houses of Lyttleton Close.
(facing page)

London in 1865.
Oil on canvas.
12×10.
The Iveagh Bequest,
Kenwood House,
London.

Sullivan aptly wrote that Houghton 'was a genially-hearted being of a loving, generous disposition, predisposed to fun, who, when hurt, hid his wounds under an added, even hysterical gaiety'. This insight into his character enables us to understand why he plunged himself into Bohemia, and travel, without regard to the consequences.

His art became that of a man haunted by the memory of his tragic loss. 'It would seem', Housman wrote, 'that a great style is hardly ever consistent with an easy philosophy of life . . . over Houghton's pictures there are apt to be shadows, and about his rendering of beauty a hush'.

The physical difficulties under which he laboured make his achievement nothing less than heroic. The loss of an eye caused him constant pain in the form of migraine headaches and severe inflammation which frequently put a stop to work for days, even weeks; he would then work at top speed to make up for lost time. This handicap dogged him for the greater part of his life, and possibly the penetrating intensity of his vision owes a great deal to the fact that he was *seeing* in spite of the suffering it caused him.

For the rest of his life he would avoid being alone as much as was possible, and made his home in clubs. And now he was back in London he resumed old friendships and made new friends. He began seeing more of his comrade Tourrier and frequented that extraordinary institution, the Society of Cogers,[3] as well as the Savage Club which he appears to have joined about this time. Both these clubs contained many of his old cronies from Leigh's, the Royal Academy Schools and the Langham.

Handsome, of little more than medium height, he dressed more like a dandy than an artist. An eyepatch concealed a blind eye, the result of a childhood accident when a playmate fired a toy cannon charged with gunpowder at his head. The injury must have made him feel self-conscious, but he overcame his sensitivity and cultivated an image around the disability, and with his bushy Bengal Cavalry beard and black eyepatch, appeared very much the genial pirate.

He possessed all the ebullient gregariousness of the Anglo-Indian, raised in a much less inhibited family circle, linked to the light-hearted gaiety of Bohemia. He

Unidentified illustration, *c*.1861. Engraved by the Brothers Dalziel. From a proof in the Print Room, British Museum, London. The model for the young girl on her deathbed was Susan; an uncanny premonition of her own early death in July 1864.

could seldom resist the temptation to take part in impromptu escapades and practical jokes. His was a typical Anglo-Saxon's sense of humour, that is, wit exerted at one's own expense, as well as at the victim's.

Bohemianism as a socio-political phenomenon originated in Paris of the First Empire when the Romantic movement spawned penniless but carefree painters, poets and journalists who with their mistresses inhabited the attics of the Left Bank, the locale of Murger's *Scènes de la vie de Bohème*. Murger's Bohemia, however, was supplanted by that of the Second Empire, a much grittier version full of social misfits, would-be writers and artists who had fallen by the wayside. Meanwhile the Murger type of Bohemia had taken root in the literary clubs and art academies of mid-Victorian London (the Second Empire version soon followed). As in France, bourgeois England had not become sophisticated enough to absorb the armies of artists and writers or to recognize their frequently innovative talents. Rebellion was the result, although in England the moderate instincts of the law-abiding middle-class were too strong to rise above the boyish pranks and high-spirited satire, before the opportunity presented itself for a successful career and respectability. In Houghton's case, it never did, yet he had, to paraphrase Joanna Richardson in her admirable survey, *La Vie Parisienne* (1971), the character to use his natural gifts, the determination to succeed, and lead a life both Bohemian and elegant.

Club life itself was a comparatively new phenomenon for artists and men-of-letters of middle-class origin. Despite its power, the middle class of mid-Victorian England was still a class apart. Men in the professions, except the Army or Navy, could still only belong to what was defined as 'society' by right of birth and family connections, while men in business could not belong to society at all. This meant that generally they were not admitted into membership of the conservative West End clubs or the homes of the aristocracy. There were exceptions, but the majority of the poets, essayists, editors and artists (often conservative as they were radical) were compelled in the sixties to frequent their own clubs and societies.

Some of these were political, having as their objective such essentially middle-class demands as parliamentary reform, extended suffrage, or the removal of various burdens on journalism, such as the Paper Duty. Some, like the Savage Club, were Bohemian and continued the Coffee House tradition of Dr Johnson's days with convivial gatherings of wits and wags; the only qualification for admission being that the prospective member was 'a working man in literature and art, and a good fellow'. The Society of Cogers, on the other hand, was avowedly political. It was founded in 1755, and was an active and flourishing club which had its origin in the tavern debating societies of the eighteenth century, when Dissenters, Unitarians and other middle-class reformers ardently discussed the democratic ideas of Tom Paine with a view to realizing them in England.

Membership of this Bohemian parliament included such literary lions as Dickens (who reputedly saw his prototype of the immortal Pickwick and other characters among the Cogers of 1834) and Mayne Reid, ex-buffalo hunter and bestselling author of Westerns; plus a diverse and lively company of thirsty freethinking actors, medical men, journalists, and, of course, artists.[4] By Houghton's time, the Cogers met at Coger's Hall, Shoe Lane, off Fleet Street, and were even more diverse, having broadened their ranks to include city merchants, civil servants and young barristers. These new recruits were eager to acquire the invaluable art of public speaking from the motley assembly of articulate literary hacks and seedy Bohemians, now reinforced by Fenians, Socialists and 'Red' Republicans.

For Houghton the most enjoyable evenings were those spent at the Savage Club. They enabled him to indulge his sense of fun at the concerts which generally followed the festive Saturday night dinners. On these occasions, artists vied with one another to give stop-gap turns between the more professional acts staged by well-known music-hall performers. These included such hardy annuals as Stacy Marks' bogus sermons and John Austen Fitzgerald's old-time Irish theatrical manager in a tizzy, supplemented by gibberish renderings of *God Save the Queen* or *Rule Britannia*. The Savage Wigwam, too, was not only an endless source of entertainment, but a practical means of contact with the interrelated worlds of Fine Arts, Literature and Journalism. Most of the younger publishers of the day were members, like

William Tinsley and Edmund Routledge, as were the Dalziels, Swain and Thomas.

Houghton met with many of the celebrated figures of his time but he never courted or cultivated them as friends. It sometimes seems that he even backed away from success, because time and time again he appeared to waste an opportunity to join the established circles. This may partly have been due to the loss of his emotional centre in Susan; so that *his* choice of friends became subjective rather than objective. The Victorian artist's wife was a vital and integral part of her husband's success: she was hostess and agent, mother, mistress and model, all at the same time. One thinks of du Maurier: certainly, without Emma, his wife and guardian angel, his life would not have been so successful in its influential social relationships.

Yet Houghton never failed to be sympathetic to the needs of his less successful fellow-artists and their dependants in times of trouble. Despite worry over his eye,

Illustration for the poem 'In Five Acts: V. The Fall of the Curtain' by Tom Taylor. Wood engraving. From *A Round of Days*, 1866. Print Room, British Museum, London. The artist depicts his parents in a tender scene drawn in 1865, shortly after Susan's death, when they had joined him and the children to live together at 162 King Henry's Road, Hampstead.

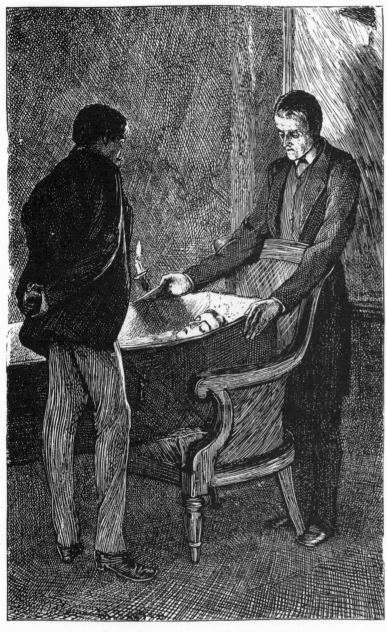

Illustration for 'Mrs Holmes Grey', by W. M. Rossetti. Wood engraving.
From *The Broadway*, 1867. Bodleian Library, Oxford.

misunderstandings with editors, publishers and engravers, and his own financial problems, he was always
ready to help. Sullivan tells the story of Mrs Henley,
wife of the illustrator, Lionel Charles Henley,[5] who had
invited someone to dinner. She and her husband particularly wanted Houghton to meet their guest. Mrs
Henley sent an urgent message by hand the same day.
The reply was that he would come, but though they
waited Houghton did not arrive until late in the evening.
He then rushed in breathless, his apology being that he
had only managed to borrow twenty pounds. The urgent
message had made him jump to the conclusion that the
Henleys were hard up.

A much more serious affair was that concerning an
early friend, Thomas Morten, who committed suicide
in September, 1866. Houghton assumed the responsi-
bilities of an executor in the absence of a will and assets,
as well as organizing a subscription for his friend's
penniless widow. He approached William Rossetti, and
became acquainted with him for the first time in October,
1866. Rossetti, then a civil servant in the Inland Revenue
Office, had many influential friends and was, into the
bargain, an important art critic. With his help, Houghton succeeded in raising £150 (*roughly £4,500 today*) for
Mrs Morten.[6]

This contact with one of the most important of Victorian art pundits brought Houghton to the notice of a
wider circle of admiring colleagues. Rossetti himself
thought him 'a man of superior quality . . . deservedly
prized as a woodcut illustrator'. He continued seeing
Houghton between 1866 and 1870 during the period of
the Morten Fund, and it is from their contact with one
another that we learn more of Houghton's continuing
eye trouble. Rossetti noted in his diary (January 26,
1869) that Houghton had told him that he was much
'less colour-blind' and wanted 'to paint, and relinquish
woodcut designing'. Characteristically, Houghton did
not take advantage of the older man's high regard for
him and his work. Rossetti states almost forlornly in
Some Reminiscences, 'I should have liked to see more of
him'. But, whenever possible, he promoted Houghton's
work by noticing his pictures in the Royal Academy of
1868 and 1869, and other exhibitions; and on at least one
known occasion, steered a commission in his direction:

a woodblock design for his long narrative poem, 'Mrs Homes Grey' (*Broadway Magazine* 2, 1868: p. 449).

Between 1860 and 1867, Houghton was also a visitor to the fortnightly Tuesday 'At Homes' of Brown in Fitzroy Square. Other visitors included: du Maurier, Morris, Mazzini, Pinwell, Prinsep, Christina and William Rossetti, Turgenev, Walker and Whistler. Rossetti introduced him to this circle with the best of intentions: nevertheless it appeared to be a milieu in which he did not feel at ease.

Du Maurier asked Pinwell to bring Houghton for lunch at his house in Great Russell Street, Bloomsbury on April 28, 1867. Du Maurier took to him at once, and 'all smoked and chatted till past four'. They had much in common, yet they never became friends in the real sense. Perhaps Emma was to blame. She may have been alarmed at Houghton's capacity for imbibing and decided that his natural charm might entice her husband back to the Bohemia she had rescued him from, forsaking the haven of refuge she so ardently desired to make for him.

No less surprising was Houghton's failure to resume contact with the ebullient and influential Marks, who had written so warmly of his early work and his promise of success. But Marks was now a successful painter, an Associate Royal Academician, and the moving spirit among the St John's Wood Clique, whose more memorable works included Yeames' *And when did you last see your father?* as well as an endless repertoire of entertainments such as comic songs and satanic pantomimes. Although Houghton certainly shared the Clique's antic humour, one can well imagine that their preference for a somewhat suspect historical past of wimpled shrews and jesters with toothache might have been too complacent for his taste. He preferred the less pretentious, less sophisticated company of those fellow-artists familiar with the face of despair. Yet within these terms he made another choice. Sympathy and understanding he found in close friends such as the bibulous Bohemian good-natured Henley. But the friend who seemed to possess all the qualities he sought, besides sharing his own approach as an artist, was Pinwell.[7]

What Houghton liked about Pinwell was his Cockney vitality and lack of pretension; that he never, for instance, tried to conceal his plebian background. There was, too, a shared sense of humanity in his work which derived a great deal from Houghton as the master. '(Pinwell) never forgot', wrote Harry Quilter in his article on the artists of the *Graphic* (*Universal Review*, 1888: p. 96-7), 'the city and its folk, and it is strange to notice in his villagers and rustics some of the hard, anxious, strained expressions which we see so surely on the faces of the London poor'. Pinwell and Houghton were good friends, though their temperaments were widely different. Yet in one respect they were united: their love and appreciation of the countryside in and around London, where, with Gilbert Dalziel, they spent much time drawing and painting. Most of Houghton's (untraced) landscapes were painted round about Hampton, Marlow and Pinner, and also Harlow, Hendon and Epping.

Also, perhaps, Houghton was drawn by the sense of impending tragedy that Pinwell emanated. The two men had not only a shared artistic vision – that peculiar combination of sadness and warmth towards humanity – but also the tragic patterns of their lives was the same. Pinwell, too, lost a young and beautiful wife after a few years of happiness. She died in 1870 of typhoid fever. He was also dogged by illness (in his case, consumption), and Pinwell and Houghton were to die within months of each other while still in their thirties.

III: Illustrator Extraordinary

In the absence of buyers for his paintings, Houghton could think of no better way to support himself and his family than to master the new woodblock medium for which there was such a growing demand. He must also have been encouraged by the fatherly concern which the Dalziels had for him. They watched over his interests at all stages, from commissioning a drawing to getting it past the editors.

Although the period in which Houghton lived has been called the Railway Age, it could, to quote de Maré, be dubbed the Boxwood Age. 'The wide distribution made possible by railways, the rapidity of the steam press, the growth of a large and literate public to whom reading was as much a habit as watching television is today, produced an enormous tide of books and periodicals. Yet when they were illustrated, as most were, the boxwood block was the only means by which pictures could be printed together with type'. These were factors which not only brought into being a generation of brilliantly talented artist-illustrators, but for the first time in England, enabled them to earn a regular income.[1]

All these periodicals were unique for their time. Wood-engraving, as applied to the making of books and magazines, was highly developed in France. By the sixties, it had reached a similar standard in Germany and the United States. But the British made most effective use of the illustrated magazine as a literary and artistic medium catering to the needs and pleasures of a home-based way of life. Eugene Benson, the Boston painter and critic, (*Atlantic Monthly* 25, 1870; pp. 681, 687) compared the English magazines to the presence of a liberal and cultivated friend, rich in the souvenirs of travel, at times eloquent, and always discreet, illuminating the minds about him, and giving a zest for knowledge. 'A home circle', he concluded, 'without such illustrated magazines is torpid and poor in its sources of

pleasure. It has neither eyes for art or nature, nor a liberal interest in anything but its routine and mechanical interest.'

This era might also be called the Dalziel Age. Before photomechanical engraving came to the rescue of long-suffering illustrators in the nineties, the Dalziels dominated the business of supplying woodblock illustrations. George and Edward Dalziel, or the Brothers Dalziel, as they called themselves, came from Newcastle. They were the pupils of the great Bewick, who had started it all by showing what could be done with the endgrain of the boxwood block. They had established a family business in London during the early 1840s, and prospered by taking whatever work came their way.

Gradually, quality superseded quantity. The publication of such landmarks of Pre-Raphaelite bookmaking as Allingham's *The Music Master* (1855), and Moxon's *Tennyson* (1857) with illustrations by Rossetti, Millais and Hunt, was the beginning. Later, they introduced the Pre-Raphaelites, Millais, Brown and Hunt, and their associates Burne-Jones and Hughes, to magazine journalism, and also their younger contemporaries, such as Walker, North, Pinwell, Sandys and Houghton.[2] Between 1855 and 1875, 'the golden decades,' nearly every illustrated book of any merit and nearly every issue of the best illustrated periodicals carried the Dalziel imprint.

The Dalziels were not the only good engravers in the field. Swain, Evans, Linton and the Whympers were of the same calibre. But the Dalziels dominated because they were also art directors, printers and publishers. They discovered young artists – usually struggling to make a name for themselves as genre painters – and as well as ensuring that they had plenty of work, they often commissioned oil or watercolour versions of the illustrations they liked and urged clients to do likewise. Such

Illustration for 'The Maid of the Woolpack', a story by Andrew Haliday. Wood engraving. From *Entertaining Things*, 1862. The British Library, London. (facing page, left)

Illustration for 'The Vision of Sheik Hamil', a poem by Isa Craig. Wood engraving. From the *Argosy*, 1866. University Library, Cambridge. (facing page, right)

sympathetic patronage, plus dedicated adherence to faithfully transcribing original designs, was exceptional.

Making a woodblock illustration was a difficult task, for there was always the danger that a drawing could be completely emasculated during the process. The artist would usually draw his illustration directly on the wood; but this would only reproduce effectively if drawn in crisply linear terms. A craftsman would then cut away the wood surface in the spaces between the drawn lines, leaving the lines in stark relief. The medium depended on the closest and most sympathetic co-operation of artist and engraver. But generally artists gave the engraver little help. One can readily sympathize with the Dalziels: not infrequently they received long overdue blocks (the prime offender being Rossetti) on which drawings had been made in ink wash, pencil, coloured chalk, *and* pen-and-ink. Yet their patience was proverbial, and the virtuosity of their craftsmen such that they could work miracles with such designs. 'We were', wrote Dalziel in a letter to White, 'constant and untiring workers with our hands, untiring because it was truly a labour of love'.

[37]

'It's a coming, and so it was.' Wood engraving. Illustration
for *The Boys of Beechwood* by Mrs Elizabeth Eiloart. 1868.
The British Library, London.

'The Woman that was a Sinner', a poem by George MacDonald.
Wood engraving. From the *Sunday Magazine*, 1870.

The Dalziel package deal proved particularly attractive for young and enterprising publishers who preferred to reserve the greater part of their capital for poaching bestselling authors and first-rate editors. One such client was a formidable young Scotsman named Alexander Strahan, who built a flourishing book and magazine empire almost overnight, and lost it in an equally startling manner about fifteen years later. He knew exactly what he wanted and had excellent taste in the printing and design of books and magazines. He was also extremely perceptive about the quality of their contents, and had, in his own words, 'at 24, quite unknown, formed a project of starting a magazine to contain not so much articles of a religious character as articles of a general character written in a religious spirit'.[3] What he started was, in fact, a lively new form of literary journalism which reflected the progressive views of the liberal clergy. Strahan's *Good Words* first appeared in Edinburgh in 1860. It became so popular that he moved publication to London and launched three more highly successful magazines, *Argosy* (1865), *Sunday Magazine* (1865), and *Good Words for the Young* (1869).

Houghton's output of illustrations, considering the shortness of his life, was enormous. He worked swiftly but seldom carelessly; the same intense deliberate observation, the same meticulous attention to significant

'Helga and Hildebrand', *c*.1865. Houghton's pencil drawing touched with white on the woodblock was photographed by the Dalziels, and transferred to another block for engraving: a practice they occasionally resorted to in order to preserve a drawing they admired. From *Ballad Stories of the Affections*. Cecil Higgins Art Gallery, Bedford.

Vignette for 'Songs of Seven', 1866.
Wood engraving. From *Poems* by Jean Ingelow.

Illustration for 'John Baptist', a poem by Edward Henry Bickersteth. Wood engraving.
$7\frac{1}{4} \times 6$. From the *Sunday Magazine*, 1868. University Library, Cambridge.

detail that preceded his early genre pictures entered into the composition of almost every drawing he made on the woodblock for engraving. The woodblock medium compelled him to visualize form in boldly massed silhouettes. And since the block could not reproduce the subtleties of drawing, his linear effects had to be achieved with a judicious combination of thick and thin brush strokes, and cross-hatched pen strokes, all in the context of a well-devised composition based on juxtaposing black shapes on white spaces.

His first step in the development of an illustration was usually a rough pencil sketch; this was followed by another more defined sketch before he traced it down on the whitened surface of the block. Finally, he would elaborate the drawing with an H degree pencil, picking out any highlights with Chinese white. His illustration technique eventually became so expert that he could go from a rough, almost shorthand sketch to a direct drawing on the block in pencil, or ink using pen or brush.

The rapid development of Houghton's style after 1862[4] indicates that he may have solved many technical problems by studying the work of Menzel, one of the greatest German painter-illustrators. Following the example of Keene and du Maurier, Houghton probably learnt much from Menzel's illustrations for Kugler's *Life of Frederick the Great* (English translation, 1843). Menzel's acceptance of the exacting limits of wood-engraving and his determination to make his illustrations more than simple decorations was as liberating and inspiring an influence as Pre-Raphaelitism. Stimulated and encouraged to explore the tradition of such draughtsmanship, Houghton also received influences from Callot, Hogarth, Keene, Millais and even Hunt. Equally important was the work of the Japanese printmakers of the *Ukiyo-E*, notably Utamaro and Hiroshige, whose work made a big impact when shown for the first time in England at the London 1862 Exhibition.

Until 1864, Houghton found illustration a natural and congenial corollary to his painting. He was used to working on a small scale; a full-page woodblock for say, *Good Words*, or for a quarto-size book, was usually about 8 × 6 (20·3 × 15·2 cms); only slightly smaller than his cabinet paintings of genre subjects, which averaged 10 × 8 (25·4 × 20·3 cms). At first, the subjects reflected his pre-

[41]

'Sister Rose', a story by Wilkie Collins. Wood engraving. From *After Dark*, 1862. The artist's first book illustration. The British Library, London.

'The Wisdom of Solomon'. An illustration for an editorial by Dr Guthrie. Wood engraving. From the *Sunday Magazine*, 1868. Houghton made many such illustrations for the appreciative Guthrie; many show the influence of Holman Hunt, although the young artist adds his own personal touches here and there.

occupation with his family. This was especially true of his early work for *Good Words*, which can be classed among the very finest examples of Victorian illustration. That they are more like prints than illustrations is due to the fact that the verses were probably written as an accompaniment.

His illustrations may be grouped under three headings: monthly magazines, books, and weekly reviews and newspapers. As well as his work for *Good Words*, he also contributed regularly to *The Quiver*, *Argosy*, *Sunday Magazine*, and occasionally to *London Society*, *Churchman's Family Magazine*, *Tinsley's Magazine*, *The Broadway*, *Every Boy's Magazine*, *Golden Hours*, and *Good Words for the Young*. Except for the *Cornhill*, he thus contributed to all the established mid-Victorian monthlies, and such famous weeklies as *Once a Week* and the *Graphic*.

In spite of accepting so much commissioned work, he was essentially his own master, and his association with periodicals was often complicated by his unwillingness to be tied down to deadlines. Sullivan writes of his unreliability in the punctual delivery of drawings, a very serious matter for a newspaper. But his expertise on the woodblock made him indispensable; the Dalziels would forgive him and turn to him again and again on every justifiable occasion.

To cope with this increasing demand, he evolved several distinctly different idioms. Occasionally he resorted to his oriental or *Arabian Nights* manner, but after 1864 he developed a slightly more realistic biblical style reminiscent of Holman Hunt, and contributed illustrations of this kind to *Once A Week* during 1866, *Good Words* during 1867, and finally to the more zealously religious *Sunday Magazine* during 1868-9, where, much to his dismay, he became one of Dr Guthrie's favourite illustrators. Between 1865-71 the *Sunday Magazine* contained something by him in almost every issue.[5]

Houghton employed a third manner for historical, usually medieval subjects associated with Protestant martyrdom, but although sometimes outstanding, these illustrations were his least successful. Guthrie was also anxious that he tackle contemporary subjects, and in 1868 and 1870 let him loose on a series of illustrations which presaged the social realism of his reportorial work

'Over wide and rushing rivers/In his arms he bore a maiden.' An illustration for 'Hiawatha', *c*.1866. Wood engraving. From *Longfellow* (Chandos Poets), 1880. The British Library, London.

Illustration for 'More About Miss Bertha'. Wood engraving. $5\frac{7}{8} \times 7\frac{1}{2}$. From the *Sunday Magazine*, 1869. University Library, Cambridge.

for the weekly *Graphic*. One of these was a superbly drawn action scene for 'More About Miss Bertha' (5, 1869: p. 513), a story about a fearless real-life social worker whom he depicts coming to the rescue of an old woman street vendor attacked by footpads, or muggers, on the 'brawling blazing' Whitechapel Road.

The challenge of this growing volume of work made Houghton an illustrator of great style and versatility. He discovered that a few dramatic contrasts of light and shadow were far more evocative than many small ones; he discovered that he could employ caricature by synthesizing facial traits, posture and costume, building them into shapes so substantial that the Dalziels would reproduce them exactly as he drew them. Perhaps from Utamaro, he also discovered that a silhouetted figure against a lightly indicated background without too much detail made a much greater impact than an evenly spread composition.

More often than not, it was the unexpected postures of his figures that gave his work its unusual quality. 'They are never posed models', wrote Sullivan, 'looking their self-conscious best, but people, real people, one feels, under some stress; and it is *their* reality and the stress which he is trying to show us, rather than the knowing application of a set convention or formula of design'. Houghton's illustrations for the Dalziels' edition of the *Arabian Nights* (1863) reveal these qualities to a remarkable extent.

One outstanding example is *The Journey of Prince Schah and the Princess of Bengal* (p. 737), a masterly design which captures the peculiar enchantment of the tales. The two figures possess extraordinary intensity and blend closely together with the strongly silhouetted flying horse, conveying the magical aura of the elopement. Although he shared the task (it first appeared as a weekly part-work) with seven other artists (including Millais, Tenniel and Pinwell), it remains very much Houghton's book, and his greatest. His eighty-seven masterly designs should have made him famous. Why they did not, except among his colleagues, remains a mystery. The very qualities that make Houghton interesting today – his subtle sense of irony and delightfully observed comment – were precisely those which made him suspect with the general public.

Study for 'The Old Gardener and Camaralzaman', 1862. Pencil. $6\frac{1}{2} \times 5\frac{3}{8}$. A working drawing, one of nine, at the Victoria & Albert Museum, London, which shows the penultimate stage woodblock illustration. Both the idea and the composition have been carefully worked out, and after obtaining the Dalziels' approval to proceed, Houghton then traced his drawing down upon the woodblock to make his final design.

'The Old Gardener and Camaralzaman'. 1863. Wood engraving. $7 \times 5\frac{3}{8}$.

'The African Magician offers New Lamps for Old', 1863.
Wood engraving. $6\frac{7}{8} \times 5\frac{1}{8}$.

'The Journey of Prince Firouz Schah and the Princess of Bengal', 1863.
Wood engraving. $7 \times 5\frac{1}{4}$.

Houghton's designs for the *Arabian Nights* signalled the beginning of a tremendously productive period of book illustration. By 1865, the Dalziel Age reached its height, as had the movement of sixties book illustration; every artist known to them appears to have been pressed into service to keep up with the illustrated book boom. Ward Lock and Tyler were the publishers of the *Arabian Nights*, but Houghton worked for as many different publishers as the Dalziels offered him. Frederick Warne participated in the popularity of the *Arabian Nights* stories by bringing out his own edition in 1866 with half of the illustrations by Houghton. Warne also published *Don Quixote* (1866), with one hundred illustrations, all by Houghton. These with their wryly humorous romanticism certainly bring out the dignified dottiness of the Don. But Houghton's more restrained characterization was overshadowed by Doré's 'Gothik' images for the Cassell edition published in the same year.

Much of his best work in book illustration appeared in the series of sumptuous volumes of verse known as Dalziel Fine Art Gift Books. These included the works of single poets as well as enormous anthologies of parlour verse, dealing with such themes as the exploits of the brave, love and marriage, the rolling deep, poverty and death. The bestselling *Home Thoughts and Home Scenes* (1865), was an anthology Houghton had all to himself with thirty-five delightful though badly-engraved illustrations.

The Dalziels also kept him busy providing occasional illustrations for new editions of established literary giants such as Dickens and Longfellow, although none of these appear to have aroused the slightest interest on the part of the respective authors. His frontispiece for Dickens' *Hard Times* (1866), in which Gradgrind acknowledges the worthlessness of his son Tom, reveals a natural affinity for Dickens' more social novels, and he would

'Thus he remained standing upright on Rozinante, tied by the wrist'. 1865. Wood engraving. (above, left)

'A day of sorrow for Sancho Panza, who was too sensible of the comforts that reigned in Don Diego's house', 1865. Wood engraving. (above, right)

[47]

'The Mock Burial', 1865.
Wood engraving. From *Home Thoughts and Home Scenes*.

have been much more suitable than other illustrators of Dickens such as Stone or Fildes. (This was followed in 1867 by another frontispiece for *Our Mutual Friend*). But for the most part Houghton was obliged to supply designs for a flood of trivia, which included nursery rhymes, histories of England, school stories with a moral uplift, stories of Christian martyrs and biblical anthologies, tales of the French Revolution, and even monthly part-works of invention and discovery.

In spite of migraine attacks and the depression following Susan's death, Houghton had, by 1869, contributed over 300 illustrations to twelve different periodicals. He had also illustrated some 35 books and three monthly part-works with a total of 500 illustrations. Some idea of the speed with which he worked may be had from an entry Rossetti made in his diary on Tuesday, November 5, 1867, the year of Doré's triumphant visit to London. Rossetti had told Houghton that he could not believe Doré's remark that he had made some 40,000 designs by the age of 29. 'He (Houghton) says that he draws his woodcut designs straight off on the block, taking as a rule, only some two to three hours per design . . . He (therefore) sees nothing incredible in the statement'.

Not surprisingly, he was weary of the task. For all his hard-won but limited success, he still cherished hopes of being something more than a woodblock illustrator, and hoped to find more time to paint. But the threat of financial insecurity kept him hard at work. He longed to quit his studio to take on a much bigger challenge: of what kind he did not know. In the summer of 1869 this came his way in the shape of a new periodical, the *Graphic*.[6]

'The Pleasures and Pains of Childhood', 1865.
Wood engraving. From *Home Thoughts and Home Scenes.*

'He stood in his black weepers and little cloak on the side of the coffin.' 'Other People's Windows': III. Wood engraving. $5\frac{7}{8} \times 4\frac{5}{8}$. From *The Quiver*, 1865. The British Library, London.

'And great ladies, sir, sends their nursemaids all the way, from Peckham to Belgravia to see the bear.' 'Other People's Windows': I. Wood engraving. $6\frac{1}{4} \times 4\frac{5}{8}$. From *The Quiver*, 1865. The British Library, London.

IV: The *Graphic*

Houghton resumed his old habit of walking the streets of London after Susan's death in 1864. And his love of popular life developed an interest in social comment.

The first indication of this appears in a series of sketches of Bad Homburg for his article on the German gambling spa for *London Society* (2, 1862: pp. 492–8). It is in these that Houghton's concern with contemporary subjects hints that he had begun to apply his essentially quizzical viewpoint to his magazine work. Three years

such an extent that it is indeed a pity that he did not illustrate the whole series.

Part II, 'The Hairdresser's Window', reported on the Victorian barber's traditional use of pet bears to encourage the fallacy that bear's grease made hair grow, and to stimulate trade, especially with the children. But this London barber, after having kept ninety-nine increasingly hungry bears, was tiring of the custom. 'They eat, sir', Friswell was told, 'four times a day, a huge bowl of

'The Gambling Rooms'. Wood engraving. Houghton's first essay in social comment was made in a style reminiscent of Richard Doyle and John Leech. From *London Society*, 1862. The British Library, London.

later he reaches a high level of invention and style in two unusual illustrations for 'Other People's Windows', a series of Mayhew-like investigations into people whose occupations are conducted behind windows, like barbers, sextons, pawnbrokers and tailors. Written by a minor Victorian man-of-letters, James Hain Friswell (1825–1878), the series ran in *The Quiver* throughout 1865. Houghton only contributed illustrations for parts II and III, but these reveal his qualities as a social observer to

rice and molasses'. Despite their popularity, they could no longer be afforded. 'It quite grieves me to kill 'em, sir'. A crowd of fascinated children is shown gazing at the carcase of the unfortunate bear, reflecting the artist's own delight in such customs.

Moving towards the other end of the social scale, Houghton executed an animated double-page foldout illustration for *London Society* (10, 1866: following p. 96), another excellent design of children entitled

'Ready for Supper'. An illustration for 'Mansion House Hospitalities'. Wood engraving. $7\frac{3}{8} \times 9\frac{1}{8}$. From *London Society*, 1866. The British Library, London.

'Ready for Supper', a scene at the Lady Mayoress' Juvenile Ball at the Mansion House. In 1868-9, the first of his scenes of contemporary life appeared in the *Sunday Magazine*. These included the dramatic design for 'Baden-Baden' (4, 1868: p. 520), a full-page illustration in a Hogarthian vein which made all the difference to the somewhat priggish criticism of Sunday gambling in German casinos. Then on December 11, 1868, his first *Graphic* illustration, *Night Charges*, was published in the second issue. This was followed by his most important contribution to the *Graphic* or any other periodical, the series, 'Graphic America', which began publication on March 5, 1870. At last, Houghton had come into his own, or so it seemed.

He had joined the *Graphic* at the right moment. By 1869, the great illustration boom had slackened off. Many artists looked elsewhere. The doyen of the movement, Millais, had found a lucrative career as a fashionable portrait painter and others quickly followed his example. Even Brown and Rossetti had found patronage

'Baden-Baden'. Wood engraving. 6 × 9¼. From the *Sunday Magazine*, 1868. University Library, Cambridge.

enough to sustain their preference for painting. Others, like du Maurier, had jumped on the *Punch* bandwagon. Most freelance illustrators longed for the psychological security of being prized as valued outside staff contributor, and even in those times such offers were not to be turned down lightly.

The *Graphic* grew out of a need for a Liberal counterpart to the Conservative *Illustrated London News*. Victorian periodicals reflected the cross-currents of social and political forces striving for power and influence; and

their importance to the cause of reform was very much greater than it is now in this multi-media age. Illustrated journalism, for example, was the achievement of the class that had been changing the face of England since the beginning of the century; the hard-working, religious, self-made men, those merchants and small landowners who were in a separate class from the aristocracy and the shopkeepers and farmers.

It must be remembered that for many years the *Illustrated London News* was radical-humanitarian and anti-

aristocratic in outlook. From 1848 its editor was the radical Charles Mackay, former assistant editor of the Whig *Morning Post*. Under his influence the *Illustrated London News* reported the wave of middle-class revolutions throughout that year; it also reported the aims and activities of the Chartists and the great emigration movement. By the sixties, however, the paper had moved to the right. Mackay departed in 1858, and its founder, Herbert Ingram, perished in 1860 in the waters of Lake Michigan whilst on a tour of the United States. Control passed to his widow, until his two younger sons, William and Charles, were old enough to take over. By then, civil war had broken out in America, and the paper had become wholly Conservative and was supporting the Confederate cause. In the course of time, as the Liberal party, too, embraced the policies of imperial expansion, the *Graphic* would travel in the same direction. But from 1869 to 1875, its policies were generally progressive; its editorial sights were set on reform and support of Gladstone.

The task of successfully launching a rival illustrated weekly was much harder than it might seem. The *Illustrated London News* was firmly established; it had pioneered picture news since 1842, and with increasing success. By 1856, circulation had reached 200,000, a remarkable figure for its day, considering that the population of the entire United Kingdom was only 20 million. Whenever a new illustrated paper showed signs of becoming a dangerous rival, the Ingrams bought it up so that the paper continued to dominate the field. Those inclined to invest in publishing ventures took the view that there really wasn't room for two picture papers. In booming Victorian England, however, this was eventually disproved.

The man who launched the *Graphic* was William Luson Thomas, a thirty-nine-year-old master-engraver who commanded both capital and resourceful management, as well as ideas to initiate new departures in style and content.[1] Basically, his innovations concerned make-up and layout as well as an improvement of engraving standards. The cardinal rule of the *Illustrated London News* had been that an engraving – unless a painting – must illustrate the text. Borrowing from *Once A Week*, Thomas made the full-page illustration independent of text, using only a series title and caption, or some brief text note, to summarize the story. Thus the picture, and the artist, were given precedence over the writer for these features commenting on social subjects. Furthermore, he increased the quality of such illustrations by not confining them to a staff of draughtsmen (as was the practice of the *Illustrated London News*), who could redraw the artist's sketch on the woodblock as an illustration, but by giving those artists who had mastered the limitations of the medium, a much wider audience.

Throughout the summer of 1869, Thomas, his partner Nathaniel Cooke, and first editor, Henry Sutherland Edwards, worked to assemble what Thomas described as 'the very best we can put together of the combination of the best writers, artists, engravers, and printers'.[2] He was, at this time, both radical and religious in his opinions. Christian responsibility was a duty. Artists, Thomas believed, could be a vital instrument to remind the reading public of that fact. Like Ruskin, he believed that art should be enjoyed as much for its closeness to life and truth as for any aesthetic qualities it might possess.

There was certainly no lack of subjects. England, most of all, London, was in ferment. De Maré tells us that:

Hordes of country people flocked into the expanding towns where . . . nothing in the way of housing or social services was organized to receive them. Every man was expected to fend for himself in the belief, based on faith rather than experience, that God helps those who help themselves. A tremendous social upheaval had occurred. Within less than a century the old quiet world of agriculture had been transformed into the humming, puffing new world of industry. Urban expansion came far too rapidly, so that for the vast majority of Londoners life was as tough and as uncertain as that in a mining camp.

It is difficult for us today to realize fully just how tough life was. The London of 1870 had 100,000 winter tramps, 30,000 paupers, and a criminal class of 16,000. It had 20,000 public houses and beer-shops frequented by 500,000 people as customers. The population of the entire city had only reached $3\frac{1}{4}$ million.

Preaching evangelical Liberalism, the early *Graphic*

'To Whom it May Concern'. Wood engraving. From *Fun*, January 26, 1867. The British Library, London. *Fun* was against the leniency shown towards embezzlers and confidence tricksters, as opposed to the harsh sentences given to common criminals.

attacked the social evils of the day, and demanded legislation. It set out to reform, to enlighten and sometimes to shock its middle-class readers. Yet it also dealt with 'all the prominent topics of the day; Literature, Arts and Sciences, Fashion and Matters interesting to the Fashionable World; Sports and Pastimes; Music, Opera, Drama'. It soon had a dazzling roll of distinguished contributors; on the literary side there were Dickens, Trollope, Reade, and Wilkie Collins. Its artists were equally celebrated: Sir Francis Grant, the President of the Royal Academy, Watts, Frith, and the former Pre-Raphaelite, Millais. But it was the hard core 'heroes' of the sixties who provided the bulk of its illustrations. The group of older men, which included Houghton, Pinwell, Charles Green, and Small, supported by a younger group – Fildes, Herkomer, Holl and Gregory – formed the essential nucleus of a freelance staff.

Each artist had the choice of his own subject, the only stipulation being that it should be of universal concern.[3] Suddenly, the darkest corners of London life began to be exposed. Fildes, the first to be published, chose a queue of shivering outcasts waiting for admission to a workhouse in his *Houseless and Hungry*; Pinwell contributed a poignant street incident entitled *The Lost Child*; Herkomer produced scenes inside lodging-houses for women, workhouses and prisons. Holl executed tableaux of almost unbearable pathos set in the great new railway stations; two notable examples being *Third Class*, and *Gone!* a heart-rending episode involving a young wife and her children, bidding an agonized farewell to a beloved husband off to try his luck in America or Australia.

Fildes, Herkomer and Holl portrayed their subjects with a skilful combination of realism and sentimentality, which today makes their pages look like backdrops to some heavy Victorian melodrama; that they led to the alleviation of misery and injustice is unlikely, but the illustrations were at once recognized as slices of the life seen or lived by millions in the booming cities, and were immensely popular. All over the world illustrated papers appeared reprinting or pirating the *Graphic*'s illustrations. This ensured overnight fame for some illustrators, Fildes for example.[4] But Houghton's *Graphic* work did not bring him comparable acclaim. He was unable to

'Early Morning in Covent Garden', 1870. Wood engraving. University Library, Cambridge.

'Night Charges on their way to Court', 1869. Wood engraving. University Library, Cambridge.

meet the public demand for such sentimental records of low life. Consequently his London scenes, although of 'universal concern', and certainly possessing 'artistic value', lacked that most vital ingredient of popular appeal: the ability to tug unashamedly at the heart-strings.

Nevertheless he contributed some of his finest illustrations of contemporary life to the *Graphic*. His first London page, *Night Charges*, appeared in the second number (December 11, 1869: p. 33), a superb design which Thomas paid the artist the compliment of engraving himself. A motley group of unfortunates have spent the previous night in convivial celebration and are being escorted along Bow Street to appear before the Magistrates' Court, and face the consequences of their uninhibited behaviour. Houghton's masterful characterization of people is revealed in a series of unsentimental but intensely human portrayals, again reminiscent of Hogarth especially in his *Rake's Progress* cycle. The respectable artisan, the young thief, the genial tart returning the banter of a greengrocer's boy, the desperate man, head bandaged, held by a pair of stalwart 'peelers', and the bored, somewhat self-conscious gentleman, not to forget the bemused constables themselves, are all very much on target.

Perhaps the drawing was received with reservation precisely because it took no moral stand, but even went so far as to condone these 'victims of vice'. The puritanical middle-class readers of the *Graphic* naturally viewed drunkenness with horror. It was a subject for a moral lesson, not light-hearted satire. Apart from Houghton's attitude, there was also the fact that the sixties style was now outdated. From 1870, such well-composed, essentially Pre-Raphaelite inspired interpretations of modern life no longer found such favour. The style was thought to be too 'aesthetic' in an increasingly materialistic age.

Yet Thomas could not dispense with an artist whose peculiar genius he had respected for so long; an artist who could not adapt his vision to the sentimental conventions of what was an increasingly commercial enterprise, well on its way to mass circulation. Houghton was not only an artist, he was an articulate, worldly man of ideas who could commit his observations to paper if need be.

These talents were soon to be realized and extended to their greatest capacities, when he took on the assignment as Special Artist in America, in a visual *tour de force* which far exceeded all expectations. As one contemporary journalist wrote, '"Graphic America" was probably the best pictorial record of a visit to a strange country which ever appeared in a newspaper'.

The Embarkation 1869. Wood engraving. $8\frac{7}{8} \times 11\frac{5}{8}$. *Graphic*, March 5, 1870.

V: To America

Thomas saw America as the 'common man's Utopia', a land of opportunity, reflecting his own preference for a democratic way of life. During 1869, the completion of two engineering marvels – the opening of the Suez Canal and the Pacific Railway, the first across America – symbolized Victorian man's capacity to triumph over the most formidable natural obstacles. Public interest ran high. Both projects had absorbed what was thought to be staggering amounts of capital and taken years to build. Once completed, however, they had brought immediate and dramatic results. The Suez Canal halved the voyage from England to India from three months to six weeks. The Pacific Railway opened up the vast reaches of the West for emigration.

Predictably, the Conservative *Illustrated London News*, more concerned with Britain's imperial mission than its investment in booming North America, dispatched its most trusted Special Artist, William Simpson, on an extended tour to report on the new route to India, the brightest jewel in the English crown. Thomas looked in the opposite direction. Aware that the Pacific Railway was built with British financial backing, he had an equally pragmatic report in mind: he would use it as a peg to hang a serial on the manners and customs of the investment, Uncle Sam himself.

It was a novel idea. For although literary celebrities, wealthy tourists and special correspondents had fallen over themselves to collect material for an endless stream of travel books, few artists had ventured to replace the traditional Yankee of *Punch* and of music-hall farces with an up-to-date version. True, English artists had made the trip across the Atlantic from time to time. Eyre Crowe had travelled in New England and the Old South with his cousin Thackeray on the lecture tour of 1852; the Scots painter, John David Borthwick, had depicted the California Gold Rush as a participant,

1851-4; Frank Vizetelly had covered the Civil War as a Special Artist, mostly from the Confederate side, for the *Illustrated London News*, 1861-5. But no English artist had, before 1869, indulged himself in leisurely observing the young nation, and crossed from East to West to depict the great democratic experiment in the latest phase of its tumultuous progress. Thomas turned to Houghton, who accepted the project without question.[1]

Published serially between March 1870 and February

The United Family of Jones 1869. Wood engraving. *Graphic*, March 19, 1870.

1873, 'Graphic America' was a triumph. The series, over 70 woodblock engravings, ranks with Doré's *London* as one of the best examples of mid-Victorian social documentary art. Houghton left Liverpool in the middle of October 1869, as a cabin-class passenger on the new Inman Line sail-steamship, *City of Brussels*. His first scenes are of the embarkation in the driving rain, and one can feel how strongly he has been infected with the mood of bustle and excitement. Everything intrigued him. The strange, wailing ditties of the sailors as they spread sail, the indefatigable energy of the habitual voyager, and not least, the grave, stoical courage of emigrants, huddled in the dark cavernous steerage. 'Theirs is, for the time

being a hard lot', he wrote, 'they must make many sacrifices to reach the promised land of plentiful work and high wages'.

Following his instinct to look behind the scenes, he descended the dark winding iron stairway into the smoky inferno of the stoke hole; 'the blaze of the furnace fires shoots out', he wrote, 'dazzling eyes and almost scorching faces'. The floor was choked with great piles of coal, which stalwart stokers heaved into the rapacious furnaces by the shovelful. His illustration, *The Stoke Hole* (March 19, 1870: p. 371) is a dramatic and strangely urgent reminder of the ceaseless sweating physical effort necessary to propel the tiny ship towards its destination.

[62]

Alfred Houghton

F. Wentworth.

The Stoke Hole 1869.
Engraved by F. Wentworth.
$11\frac{3}{4} \times 8\frac{3}{4}$. *Graphic*,
March 19, 1870.

In the steerage, the fine weather had enticed the emigrants from their gloomy quarters for much-needed fresh air and sunshine. To cabin-class passengers, these less-privileged folk were a constant source of entertainment. Germans, Russians and Irish brightened the steerage area with their strange fur hats and brightly-coloured kerchiefs. Houghton depicted the scene in *Steerage Emigrants* (March 19, 1870: p. 368). Some cabin-class passengers kept themselves occupied watching the oiling of the binnacle, while another group clustered about the big red funnel, smoking and talking politics. Others immersed themselves in the ship's library or played chess or whist. Shipboard romances flourished; 'by rights', observed Houghton, 'the ocean steamer should be the matchmaking dowager's paradise'.

One day, shortly after dawn, early risers with spy

glasses spotted a narrow film of land, looking like a dim irregular line drawn over the water. Down on the steerage deck, emigrants shouted, '*America!*' and jostled one another to catch a glimpse of the New World they had set their hopes on. Cabin-class passengers laid bets of champagne suppers at the Astor, on whether the number of the oncoming pilot-boats would be odd or even. Fashionable couples disappeared to change from travelling clothes into more elegant attire. By the time the ship entered the Narrows – the harbour entrance between Brooklyn and Staten Island – everyone was on deck, tightly packed against the rails. The scene was amazing. The enormous harbour of the Inner Bay had come into full view. Docks were crowded with tugs, oyster-boats, schooners and ferries. 'Long double-decked steamboats sped swiftly by us', wrote the artist, 'crossing and re-crossing our path, with their festooned awnings, gilded figureheads and huge revolving paddles'. Rising on the skyline were the office buildings of lower Manhattan.

The *City of Brussels* disembarked its long-suffering passengers in New York harbour during the afternoon of October 24, 1869. Houghton then spent the rest of October and half of November drawing New York life before visiting the Shaker Village at New Lebanon, Boston, Syracuse and Niagara Falls, the limit of his travels in the East. A note in the *Graphic* (January 29, 1870: p. 215) informed the readers of his itinerary: 'Mr Houghton is on his way from the Strand to San Francisco by the Union Pacific route, calling at Liverpool and New York, and visiting the Shakers at Lebanon and the Mormons at Great Salt Lake City, and returning east via the Southern States'.

A total of 72 drawings were engraved out of a probable 100 or more taken back to England. The note added that 'Mr Houghton's drawings will be accompanied by an appropriate text'. Often these were bowdlerized to soften the effect of more critical comments (particularly concerning some aspects of New York). At best, however, the artist's supporting text gives us a great deal of his very personal way of looking at places. The 'one-eyed artist in America', as he called himself in his pocket sketchbook, missed very little, and produced a remarkably complete visual and verbal account of post-Civil War America.

Off Queenstown 1869. Wood engraving. *Graphic*, March 12, 1870.

To be in New York in 1869 was to be at the nerve-centre of American life. And the city immediately impressed Houghton with its raw and restless vitality. He noted that everything was so 'showy', from the vast marble palaces of wholesale dry goods merchants, to shops and theatres. Signboards were enormous, often covering the houses in huge bold letters. The people were brisk and go-ahead, the city explosively busy – 'so very new', but 'unsubstantial-looking compared with Europe'.

The Fifth Avenue Hotel (on Madison Square) where he stayed was a celebrated hostelry of the Gilded Age. No other hotel could match it for its exuberant atmosphere of unbridled confidence.[2] It was unlike anything the worldly artist had experienced before, and staying there was clearly an ordeal until he could feel at his ease, and become accustomed to the constant 'clatter and

The Dust Barrel Nuisance 1869.
Wood engraving.
Graphic, March 26, 1870.
(left)

New York Nursemaids 1869.
Wood engraving.
Graphic, March 26, 1870.
(right)

bustle and noise, all-rushing and loud-talking and bell-ringing, all-crowding and hurrying and ceaseless confusion'. The hotel's luxurious barber-shop, crowded with its successful and flamboyant out-of-town clientele 'at nine in the morning', prior to setting out for the day's business or pleasure, provided Houghton with one of his first subjects, *Barber's Saloon, New York* (April 16, 1870: p. 465). It is an extraordinary image which captures the showy transient quality of American hotel life, pushed almost to the point of a nightmare by means of a slight exaggeration. Houghton had the ability to take realism to the edge of the grotesque, and in this case all he uses is the contrast between the immensely tall man standing up to be brushed and his squat and burly Negro attendant.

Other than sustaining necessary contact with colleagues,[3] Houghton appears to have taken little interest in socializing with polite New York society. As was his habit in London, he went his own way, to allow his experiences and adventures to take their course in the company of ordinary or less conventional people. He did not have to go far; outside his hotel, or in short walking distance, was all the material he needed to put his uncannily observant eye to work. He walked down Broadway, by the 'brilliant and many-sized shops, the high marble palaces, marts of merchant princes'. The scrambling pandemonium of vehicles reminded him of Oxford Street in London:

There is the same steady tide of human beings, flowing in the morning, toward the business quarter, and at sundown flowing uptown again; only these are perhaps, more eager and careworn faces – well-dressed men of property who are restless to learn the price of stocks; frail, scantily-clad girls, too soon shrivelled by want, who are hurrying to their shirt-making or their counter-tending.

Barber's Saloon, New York 1869. Wood engraving. $8\frac{5}{8} \times 11\frac{3}{4}$. *Graphic*, April 16, 1870.

New York Police 1869.
Wood engraving.
Graphic, March 26, 1870.

New York too, had the 'London-like passion' for business. Speculation flourished like a virulent disease. On Wall Street, he found, fortunes were made or lost in 'perpetual War of Mammon'. As in London, 'The Goddess of Commerce', he observed, 'holds an absolute and undisputed sway', but in New York, 'she becomes an avenging deity, a Juggernaut crushing devotees and victims beneath relentless wheels'. This was a reference to the events which followed September 24, 'Black Friday', 1869, when the intrigues and counter-intrigues of Jay Gould and Jim Fisk precipitated a sordid currency scandal ($11 million profit from cornering the gold market). In the Gold Room, just below the Stock Exchange, Houghton found himself watching a frenzied battle between the bulls, who were trying to force up the price of gold, and the bears, intent on bringing it down.

[68]

The scene is a more startling illustration of human passion than you ever see depicted on the stage, even though it be Othello raging or Lear wandering crazy in the Tempest [*sic*]. You see men shouting till their veins swell and their faces are purple; tearing their hair, weeping, laughing, grinding their teeth, and clenching their fists. Now a man starts off exultant, shaking a bundle of precious papers over his head; then another rushes from the hall, his face hidden in his hands, and you hear him mutter hoarsely that he is 'ruined'.

Houghton left 'this unhealthy, feverish air' to take a turn about the teeming wharves of the North River. After watching the palatial, double-decked steamboats loading up for departure to Boston, and the ferries to Jersey City and Hoboken, he retraced his steps up Broadway again, bound for the 'fashionable uptown

quarter', around the Fifth Avenue Hotel. Here he found another subject, an unemployed Civil War veteran, one of the many demobilized Union soldiers, whose jobs had gone, along with their health and limbs. Such unfortunates were unable to adjust to a changed labour market, and this veteran was soliciting money from the well-heeled crowd with the help of a child organ-grinder. Houghton depicted him glaring with undisguised

Studies of cab-drivers, for *New York Police* 1869. Pencil. $4\frac{5}{8} \times 3$. From the artist's sketchbook in the Print Room, Victoria & Albert Museum, London.

Ladies Window at the New York Post Office 1869. Wood engraving. $8\frac{7}{8} \times 7\frac{7}{8}$. *Graphic*, April 23, 1870.

hostility at a pair of wealthy widows in black mourning clothes. He called the drawing *New York Veils* (April 2, 1870: p. 419), but whether he intended the scene to portray the pathos of the aftermath of the Civil War or not, the gulf between rich and poor, the fortunate and the unfortunate, was poignantly revealed with haunting irony.

But however much he had become aware of the ten-

sions of New York City and its strident brand of rampant materialism, it was not until he had fully exposed himself to both the light and the shadows that he realized that from what he had seen so far, America was certainly no earthly paradise.[4]

Houghton also chose to comment on that American spectacular, the midnight torchlight parade. Later he explored the sprawling shantytowns and teeming tenements which lay behind the dazzling emporia and ornate Fifth Avenue mansions. A day before the torchlight parade, he had called on Charles Parsons.[5] No doubt the kindly art editor of *Harper's Weekly* gave him a warm welcome at his office in Franklin Square; Houghton was after all, the first English illustrator of note to visit New York. *Once a Week*, *Good Words* and the *Sunday Magazine* sold almost as many copies in the eastern United States as in England. He may have suggested to Houghton that he watch the big event of the week: Tammany Hall's celebration of the successful election of their candidate for Governor of New York: a midnight parade.[6]

Houghton had arrived during Grant's first term of office; the heyday of the robber barons and the big grafters. Reconstruction and a booming economy went hand in hand with corruption, but the latter had a Midas touch. Senators and Congressmen and Councilmen were being bought and sold like merchandise; graft even entered the White House. We may draw a parallel with America of the 1970s. There were, of course, many Americans who did not remain indifferent, and Fletcher Harper, the Republican owner of *Harper's Weekly*, was one of them (at least as far as Democratic corruption was concerned). The *Weekly* was, therefore, in the forefront of the fight to expose Boss Tweed, a Democrat, and his infamous Ring, busily mulcting the city treasury out of one dollar for every two paid out. Thomas Nast's scathing anti-Tammany cartoons had appeared weekly in the paper throughout 1869 and the campaign against the Ring and its control of the Mayor and city government was increasing in intensity.

The parade was, in the words of the *New York Herald* (October 28, 1869) 'magnificent'. Tens of thousands marched up Broadway to Union Square and around Madison Square, then back to Tammany Hall. 'The city', wrote Houghton, 'is in a perfect hurly-burly of uproar and excitement (and) there is a continual pandemonium of noises and yelling, and hurrahing and hissing'. It was indeed a most dramatic spectacle which provided the artist with an opportunity to deploy his best satiric manner.

Tammany Democratic Procession in New York (March 26, 1870: p. 396) appeared as a full-page engraving. This illustration was the first indication of how uncompromisingly Houghton was looking at the American and his way of life, and it must have made Thomas uneasy about what was to follow. Here was the face of the powerful machine holding the city to ransom. American readers protested, and well they might if they were Democrats. Finely composed and boldly critical in its questioning of the Tammany political juggernaut, it is a mixture of symbolism and documentary illustration; a remarkably apt use of the modern morality, or comic history picture in the context of pictorial journalism. Drummer boys lead a sinister double line of fur-hatted German, Irish, Italian and Jewish marchers, armed with battle-axes and wearing the uniforms of an English Guards regiment. Behind, another group of Tammany runners and ward heelers wearing Indian costume, carry rifle torches which eerily illuminate their villainous faces against the darkness. In the far background, a brass band performs brassily, wildly silhouetted against another marching column of torchbearers. Above it all, Liberty or Columbia, under her canopy topped by a gilded eagle, expresses grave doubts about the whole farcical charade.

But even stronger criticism would greet Houghton's downright account of his visit to Five Points,[7] a vast citadel of the poor (mostly Irish), the dissolute and the criminal, a stone's throw from crowded Broadway east of Worth Street. Like most English travellers, he was prompted to compare it with the worst London had to offer, the rookeries of Seven Dials in St Giles. It was the most dangerous and deprived quarter of Manhattan. There was a difference, however. Five Points was a precursor of the Lower East Side of the nineties in that it was also the refuge of thousands of unfortunate emigrants (at this time mainly German and Irish) who had relied too much on providence, or had been swindled and robbed almost as soon as they landed. New York was indeed an emigrant's city. But nothing could be further from their dream of the promised land. When Houghton mixed with a community of German and Irish ragpickers, however, he was surprised to find that some still had every intention of going west with what they could save by their gleaning.

The Republican *Harper's Weekly* found it difficult to forgive Houghton. Later, in 1872, when they published

Tammany Democratic Procession in New York 1869. Wood engraving. $8\frac{7}{8} \times 11\frac{3}{4}$. *Graphic*, March 26, 1870.

two of his Western pictures, with due acknowledgements this time, comment was made on 'Graphic America' as a series. While admitting that many of Houghton's illustrations were 'effective and truthful because his prejudices were not involved', the *Weekly* asserted that when Houghton was in New York, 'he either wilfully perverted what he saw, or else had a singular faculty for seeing what was not observable to ordinary eyes'.[8]

Such a viewpoint reflected the American sensitivity to any adverse British opinion of its image and institutions; and after the Civil War, to what was felt to be the condescending, if not hostile attitude of the British upperclass traveller. Yet one also wonders if Houghton's refusal to sentimentalize hadn't a great deal to do with

In the Rag Trade 1869.
Engraved by W. L. Thomas.
Graphic, April 9, 1870.

The Tombs 1869.
Wood engraving. $11\frac{1}{2} \times 8\frac{3}{4}$. *Graphic*, April 9, 1870.

it. Doré's *London*, although questioned on various points of accuracy, was never subjected to the kind of criticism heaped on Houghton's New York. Doré was extremely shy (unusual for a Victorian artist) and when he had to sketch people in the streets of London, invariably asked his collaborator, Blanchard Jerrold, to stand in front to conceal him. ('We were spies upon (people)', wrote Jerrold). But with Houghton, one senses that he confronted people face to face; he was not afraid of them, nor of what he saw, and being candid to such a degree made the result much more liable to criticism.

Almost conveniently situated in the heart of Five Points were the dark and forbidding Halls of Justice, nicknamed 'The Tombs'. The prison was only used for those charged with the gravest offences. Inside the narrow, lofty hall of the male section, stove-heated to the point of suffocation, Houghton remained only long enough to make the slightest notes of the furnace-like doors of the cells and the subdued demeanour of relatives talking to the inmates. Yet what he saw remained vividly in his mind and he created a stark and tragic illustration, *The Tombs* (April 9, 1870: p. 436). It is an image as remarkable for its humanity no less than for its highly effective composition; against the absolute whiteness of the prison gallery are the dark huddled figures of grief-stricken women talking to their unfortunate sons, brothers or husbands, condemned to death in this funereal place.[9]

Shortly before Thanksgiving Day – the last Thursday in November, 1869 – Houghton left New York for Boston, arriving in the midst of an old-fashioned snowy New England winter. Leaving Boston on the Boston and Albany railroad, he stopped off at Pittsfield in the Berkshire Hills of eastern Massachusetts to make a pilgrimage to the Shaker Village some three miles away at Mount Lebanon. Here he found a very different America: the country of those who had rejected the concept of the survival of the fittest as alien to their Christian faith and had founded communes to propagate the blessings of security, discipline and selflessness. Again, it all sounds vividly like the mood of a later America, when thousands of young Americans decided that they, too, had had a surfeit of social unrest and economic greed, and of the reduced quality of life which resulted from it.

[74]

VI: Mother Ann's Commune

The Shaker Village at Lebanon Springs lay near the north-eastern boundary of New York, within a short distance of the line which divides that state from Massachusetts, 150 miles north of New York City. Houghton found it an unreal contrast. The Georgian-style buildings of the settlement (now occupied by the Darrow Boys' School) were surrounded by gently rising hills and beautiful verdant valleys: six thousand acres of rich fertile soil. Here, within the context of an America fast losing its rural characteristics, thoughts and practices had been established which paralleled Christian Socialism, as well as ideas and principles held by himself, the evangelical Strahan and the Quaker Dalziels. Deeply fascinated, Houghton devoted a series of six illustrations to the Shaker Commune and its activities.

The Shakers had appeared nearly a century before, in 1774. They were an astonishing body of people, led by an English factory girl, Ann Lee, the 'mother' of this, the first successful religious commune in America. They called themselves the United Society of Believers in Christ's Second Appearing; but to the outside world their emotional meetings, during which members shook and danced in religious frenzy, had given them the name of the Shaking Quakers, or simply Shakers.

Mother Anne Lee was the alienated wife of a lusty Manchester blacksmith. Her tragic experiences of giving birth to (and losing) four children in horrendous agony not only undermined her health, but caused her to seek an escape from the grim realities of eighteenth century sex, and find satisfaction in the fantasy of her personalized religion. The sect was conceived in her visions and nightmares. Mother Ann's doctrine was simple: confession was the door to the new life, celibacy its rule and cross. The world's evils – war, disease, famine, poverty, the inequality of the sexes, depravity – all were the result of fleshly lust. The mission of the true church was to expose such vices, and to demonstrate how salvation could be achieved on earth once one was free of this bondage.

Between the visions and their final realization stretched many years. Mother Ann tried to plant the seed first in England but was persecuted and imprisoned. She and her flock then emigrated to America and settled in New York, and were persecuted again. They proceeded to New England, where they were beaten, imprisoned and even raped before establishing communes of poor settlers in Maine, New Hampshire and Connecticut. Finally they settled at New Lebanon, where Mother Ann died in 1785. Among her survivors was a formidable group of 'Elders' led by Joseph Meacham, the first builder of Shaker Communism.

Though governed by an essentially romantic ideal, the Shakers soon became down-to-earth New Englanders. By 1789, a tannery, clothing shop, chair factory, a blacksmith and a cobbler's shop were going full blast. A Shaker garden-seed industry was started, as was a highly organized agriculture which included stockbreeding, beekeeping and every kind of crop from potatoes to parsley. Despite the obvious handicap of celibacy, Shakerism attracted an increasing stream of God-fearing idealists, poor farmers and emigrant artisans escaping from marital problems, broken homes and fear of big cities.[1] The movement became much more social under the influence of such leaders as the economist Daniel Fraser, the son of a Paisley silk weaver, who held very definite ideas about 'universal' ownership of the land and corresponded with Ruskin[2]; James Prestcott, an early advocate of eugenics; and foremost among them, Frederick Evans, a forceful radical whose ideas on political reform, sanitation, dietary reform and scientific agriculture were well ahead of their time.

Evans, who had come to America from England in

Shaker Evans at Home 1869.
Wood engraving.
$8\frac{7}{8} \times 11\frac{7}{8}$.
Graphic, August 26, 1871.

The Religious Dance 1869.
Wood engraving.
$8\frac{7}{8} \times 11\frac{7}{8}$.
Graphic, May 14, 1870.
(facing page, above)

Study for *The Religious Dance*
1869. Pencil. From the artist's
sketchbook in the Print Room,
Victoria & Albert Museum,
London. (facing page, below)

1820, had thrown in his lot with the Shakers in 1830. He had been associated with his brother, George Henry Evans, in the publication of several populist journals which propagated such principles as the right of every man to vote himself a farm, equal rights for women, the abolition of chattelism, wage slavery and imprisonment for debt. The indefatigable Evans continued to campaign for these and other reforms, shrewdly relating them to Shakerism. He corresponded with Henry George on the single tax; with Tolstoy on co-operation and non-resistance. He lectured, wrote articles and invited the world to visit Mount Lebanon.

Houghton was not only the first English artist to visit New Lebanon but one of the very few artists to be given the facilities to depict Shaker activities. His illustrations, therefore, assume added importance historically. He made sketches for a series of large woodblock drawings depicting three successive episodes of a Shaker evening meeting. The first of these, published as *Shaker Evans at Home* (August 26, 1871: p. 213) depicted the Shaker chief opening the service by preaching extempore from the Bible. Fraser is probably the Elder sitting on the immediate right of Evans.

Shakers at Meeting: The Religious Dance (May 14,

1870: p. 556) was the second episode. After the sermon and hymns all would then be told to go forth and worship God in the dance, 'believing that', wrote Houghton, 'like Miriam and David, they should manifest their religious exultation and gratitude to God by sacred dances and joyous psalmody'. The dance, called the Gift of Love, provided a dramatic and enchanting climax:

> the meeting forms into lines for dancing, the women on one side, the men on the other. They are holding their hands out with the palms upward, as if waiting to catch the grace and blessing of the Deity. The

[77]

women are kissing each other, and whispering in each other's ears, doubtless confessing their faults or consoling a sister who has thought herself guilty of some offence against God; while one elderly sister has laid her hand tenderly on a little girl's head – the little damsel does not seem quite to comprehend what it is all about – and is evidently bestowing her blessing upon her.

Young and old are mixing freely together, and as the dance goes on, the good people grow more and more earnest, and their voices tremble and quaver as they sing.

The third illustration, *The Final Procession* (May 14, 1870: p. 557) was the Solemn March of the Final Procession and the closing rite of the meeting. It was:

performed with great gravity, and the faces have a most solemn and devout expression. However one may be disposed to make sport of these quaint attitudes and notions, he is speedily, if he has any sin-

cerity, checked in this feeling, when he sees how deeply earnest and sincere are the good people, who look upon this as the true way of manifesting their devotion and their gratitude to God.

Utterly different from the ritual of worship, with its odd atmosphere of mystical sensuality, was the tranquil daily life of the commune. The meetings with their hymns and dances were a welcome release. Outside, in the fields, the workshops and the frame houses, Shaker religion took the form of a zealous devotion to utilitarian pursuits. 'The Shaker hive', wrote Houghton, 'permits no drones'.

The 'North Family' which comprised sixty men, women and children, inhabited three spacious, roomy, well-built frame houses. 'All the family are out of bed at half-past four in the morning (half an hour later in winter), have their breakfast at sharp six, dine at noon, sup at six again, and retire about ten'. Attached to their houses were workshops, barns, storehouses and outhouses for the various animals. Each brother and sister could choose the kind of work he had most taste and aptitude for, with skilled craftsmen in every trade. Houghton thought that this thrift and free choice of occupation was the foundation of the settlement's prosperity.

Social peace and harmony prevails among (the) cabinetmakers and carpenters, farmers and shepherds, ironsmiths and silversmiths, architects and tailors, among the brethren; and among the sisters, cooks, seamstresses, straw-workers, bonnet-makers, and schoolteachers.

Strangely enough, *Shaker Evans at Home* brought much the same reaction as had his Broadway Squad and the Five Points ragpicker. The illustration was reprinted in *Harper's Weekly*, but this time protest came not from readers but from the portrayed, Elder Frederick Evans himself. Incensed by what he imagined to be unfriendly caricature, he called on the editors to, in Abbey's words, 'kick up a row about Houghton's picture of him'. Houghton could not adapt his vision of America to *any* of the conventions of the time! Yet it is obvious that Houghton (despite whatever reservations he may have had about Evans) intended his Shaker series to be a gentle affectionate chronicle. Briefly, he had stepped out

The Final Procession 1869. Wood engraving. 8¾ × 11⅞. *Graphic*, May 14, 1870.

Shaker Sleighing Party 1869. Wood engraving. *Graphic*, May 7, 1870.

News Room, Boston Athenaeum.
Wood engraving.
Published as *Boston News Room*.
Graphic, April 30, 1870.
(above, right)

Study of readers in the artist's
hotel, Boston. Pencil.
From the artist's sketchbook
in the Print Room, Victoria
& Albert Museum, London.

Police Convoy in Boston 1869.
Wood engraving. *Graphic*, May 7,
1870 (facing page)

of time to depict the life-style of a plain people whose ideas found such remarkable expression in Utopian enterprise.

Before visiting the Shakers, Houghton had spent some three weeks in Boston.[3] In common with all American cities of the East, Boston had mushroomed rapidly since Dickens' first visit in 1842. It was now a city of a quarter of a million people. But the 'Athens of America' still possessed its 'air of literary refinement and elegant hospitality', which had so impressed the young novelist. Houghton was given a conducted tour and he wrote at length of his impressions of Harvard, 'whose scholarly sphere is so clearly felt', the beautiful townships of Milton, Roxbury and Quincy 'retreats of the studious, professional men and prosperous votaries of commerce and trade'. He was also shown the new Public Library in Boylston Street, and the State Street Exchange (April 30, 1870: p. 512). He climbed the Bunker Hill monument on Breed's Hill and explored the picturesque streets of Beacon Hill.

Such sightseeing provided him with little pictorial material. He had no interest in landscape architecture without the involvement of people. But a heavy fall of snow on November 17 turned Boston into a wonderland, and fired his imagination. Once more he was able to create lively significant images of hurrying citizens and horse-drawn sleighs, all of which reveal his own personal

enjoyment of winter as a purely visual experience. Blown hither and thither by what he described as 'a boreal guillotine', he sank into snowdrifts, bumped into housegates, and fought to maintain his balance on the precipitous slopes which led to Cambridge and Charles Streets from Beacon Hill. The number and speed of sleighs made street-crossing dangerous. And in *Police Convoy in Boston* (May 7, 1870: p. 533), a superb design, he portrayed with great gusto the genial courtesy of a protective policeman escorting the prettiest girls across the traffic of fast-moving sleighs on snowbound Cambridge Street. (As far as is known there were no complaints from readers about him.) Towards the Common, the snowstorm had blocked traffic completely, but, wrote Houghton, 'Yankee energy soon sets it free again'. A snow plough made its appearance, 'a great cumbersome, wooden affair', and in another three-quarter page, *A Boston Snow Plough* (April 30, 1870: p. 513), he evokes all the bustle and excitement of the occasion with a most telling balance of black to white.

[80]

Study for Boston Snow Plough
1869. Pencil. From the artist's
sketchbook in the Print Room,
Victoria & Albert Museum,
London. (above, left)

Study for young woman in
Boston Pets 1869. Pencil.
Detail from the artist's
sketchbook in the Print Room,
Victoria & Albert Museum,
London. (above, right)

Boston Pets 1869.
Wood engraving. 6 × 9.
Graphic, April 30, 1870.

Boston Snow Plough 1869. Wood
engraving. *Graphic*, April 30,
1870 (facing page)

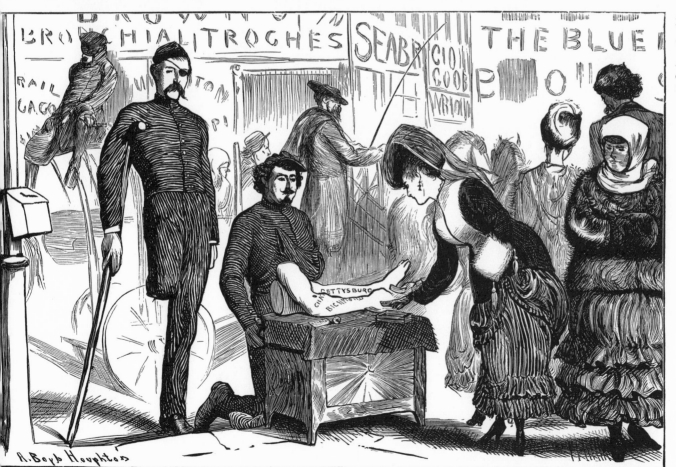

Frog Town Rangers 1869. Engraved by Swain. 8⅞ × 11⅞. *Graphic*, April 2, 1870.

A contrast to such boisterous events was seen on the south end of Tremont Street, adjacent to the Common, where he was again confronted with a reminder of the late Civil War; the spectacle of two maimed survivors, 'reduced to charity for their subsistence'. The following week, shortly before leaving Boston, he celebrated Thanksgiving at Christ Church, Cambridge, and viewed the Thanksgiving Parade on Cambridge Common. It was an unusual spectacle: a mounted cavalcade of 'raga-muffins' in every imaginable disguise. Indian chiefs were the favourite, but there were Turks and gypsies, dragoons and generals, imps and Irishmen, crusaders and kings, Yankees and broad-brimmed Puritans.

Houghton, who always loved the grotesque quality of folk festivals, was delighted, and made pencil drawings for his equally unusual full-page *Frog Town Rangers* (April 2, 1870: p. 419). The passion for such masquer-ades and burlesques, he was told, had crossed the Atlan-tic from England some years before. Since then, college students had taken delight in initiating freshmen into secret societies, with all the honours of 'costly, ludicrous and terrifying disguises'. So, too, it had become custom-ary to parody patriotic celebrations of various anniver-saries such as the Fourth of July, Thanksgiving, and Washington's birthday.

Leaving Boston by train on the Boston and Albany, he stopped off at Pittsfield to make his visit to the Shakers. After staying at New Lebanon for three days he went on to Syracuse. He found his next stop, Buffalo, a great deal less elevating. Although suitably impressed by Niagara's roar, he was pestered by touts, gatekeepers and hordes of Seneca squaws selling beadbags and moccasins; he could think of no greater contrast to the Niagara Falls of Frederick Church's romantic imagination.[4] Particularly disillusioning was his first contact with the American Indian. Instead of the tall, erect figures of bronzed and comely countenance promised by Cooper and Long-fellow, he saw at Niagara hordes of dirty and dejected blanket Indians, selling souvenirs, or worse still, begging for small coins. 'Romance', he concluded, 'oozes out of you as fast as your shillings current and pounds sterling'.

Boston Police 1869. Wood engraving. *Graphic*, April 30, 1870.

VII: Going West

In early January 1870 Houghton set out on the second part of his American Odyssey with a deep sense of relief. Like many sensitive Americans at that time, notably Twain and Nast, he had felt impelled to comment on a society whose idealism had all but disappeared under an avalanche of money. Perhaps a trip across the continent would enable him to forget the fevered East.

To the more romantic traveller, the frontier west was the meeting-point between savagery and civilization. Going west, therefore, was what appealed most to Houghton. There he would see if the America of his boyhood dreams, created by the romances of Cooper and Longfellow, and heightened by the pictorial chronicles of Catlin, were reality or myth.[1] The transcontinental railroad track had been open for less than a year. The state of Nebraska was only three years old. Colorado, the Dakotas, Wyoming, Montana and Utah had not yet been admitted to the Union. California had come of age, a state now twenty-three years old. And fortunately for Houghton, his visit coincided with a brief interval of peace on the Western plains. The Bozeman Trail, through Nebraska and Wyoming to the goldmines of Montana, which had touched off a Sioux uprising (Red Cloud's War) had been closed since 1867.

He boarded a transcontinental passenger train at the Jersey City depot of the Pennsylvania Railroad. It would take him two weeks to reach Omaha, the terminal point of the Pacific Railroad. The first leg of his journey to Cincinnati would have taken him twenty-six hours; first to Philadelphia, then along the line of the Baltimore and Ohio Railroad, through Baltimore itself and the Point of Rocks, the precipitous cliffs of Elk Mountain, and beside the tumultuous passage of the Potomac River, through the Blue Ridge Mountains. As the train made its way through Pennsylvania and along the Cumberland Valley, the landscape grew wilder. At Harper's Ferry the train entered the Shenandoah Valley of West Virginia;

How differently do the wide-spreading and somewhat straggling Virginia farms look from the cosy, limited hedgebound domains of Old England! You see strange growths; wonder what the red delicate flower of the buckwheat is, and admire its beauty; are struck by the high Indian corn, with its thick knotted stalks, and its long, rough, drooping leaves, and its thick ears, from which hang the skeins of natural silk, soft, glossy, and floating in the slightest breeze; the water-melon vines, with their exquisitely-shaped leaves, and the great long green water-melons.

Houghton caught a glimpse of the tensions of the 'Reconstructed' South. Emancipation had been made part of the Constitution. The Freedmen's Bureau had opened Negro schools, relief centres and special courts. Throughout the South, Negro suffrage was made legal. Yet what Houghton saw made him feel that, visibly at least, abolition of slavery had done little to change the Southern Negro or his lot.

War swept over this country, and you see here and there vestiges of its rage and fury in desolate farms and deserted villages. At the little wooden, shabby and broken-down stations at which you stop, groups of ragged darkies of all ages and sizes look upon you from under tattered straw hats, and out of big, yellow-balled staring eyes, not very different, apparently, from what Negroes were before amendments of the Constitution made them not only men and brothers but citizens armed with the full power of citizenship and suffrage. They look as seedy and as lazy, are as fond of slouching about and going to sleep, as ever, and the plantations round about betray how little the abolition of slavery has improved Virginian thrift.

The whites who you see, too, are an indolent, lazy-

Pig-Driving in Cincinatti 1869. Wood engraving. *Graphic*, July 9, 1870.

On Board A River Steamer 1869.
Wood engraving.
$5\frac{7}{8} \times 9$.
Graphic, July 9, 1870.

Study of Miss Betsa McPherson,
Tuscola, 1869. Pencil.
Inscribed 'Bedmaker,
McPhersons, Tuscola'. Detail
from the artist's sketchbook
in the Print Room, Victoria
& Albert Museum, London.

going set; they have wide-brimmed hats and long hair, and sunburnt, hatchet faces; their hands are plunged deep into their pockets, they are puffing at native cigars and cornstalk pipes, their apparel is Virginian homespun, and their manners clearly Virginian homebred. A few you may see of the sharper, more wide-awake, money-making sort; Northern men who have strayed hither to settle, have bought up unoccupied farms on the free labour system, and go to Congress by the aid of Negro votes. These are the carpet-baggers, of whom you hear so much in the political circles of American cities. They do not seem to be on the best of terms; the carpet-bagger despises his Southern neighbour because the latter does not make money, and the (white) native hates the carpet-bagger because he does.

At Cincinnati he boarded an express steamer of the United States Mail line which was to take him west on the Ohio to Louisville and Cairo, and then north up the Mississippi to St Louis. It was an adventurous voyage of three days and nights. 'The great snorting steamboats', wrote Houghton, 'have a chronic propensity for racing, and occasionally send their machinery and passengers into the air together'.

In St Louis, before continuing his journey westward to Chicago, he stopped to present his letters of introduction and collect the necessary papers from General Sherman's military headquarters. These would enable him to visit and stay at army posts and Indian reservations. His visit to Chicago was almost as brief. (Early Chicago vied with New York in the scale of its corruption.) But he dutifully inspected the notorious lockup under the Old Town Hall, and paid visits to the Mercy Hospital and the city's pride and joy, the Union Stockyards. The richest and fastest-growing city of the West could not be ignored, so he put four quarter-page illustrations on to woodblocks.

He also visited General Sheridan's headquarters for

Study for *Rag Collectors* 1869.
Pencil. $4\frac{5}{8} \times 3$. From the artist's
sketchbook in the Print Room,
Victoria & Albert Museum,
London.

Rag Collectors 1869.
Wood engraving.
Graphic, April 9, 1870.

Scene in the Prison at Chicago 1869. Wood engraving. *Graphic*, July 9, 1870. The
artist depicts himself inspecting the notorious cells under the old Town Hall.

Sisters of Charity in Chicago 1869. Wood engraving. *Graphic*, July 16, 1870.

A. Boyd Houghton

Coasting at Omaha 1870. Engraved by Swain. $8\frac{7}{8} \times 11\frac{7}{8}$. *Graphic*, January 19, 1871.

help in arranging the services of William F. 'Buffalo Bill' Cody, for a hunting expedition he wanted to make on the Great Plains. More than likely, it was through Sheridan that he met Lord Flynn, as the celebrated Anglo-Irish sportsman appears in Houghton's quarter-page illustration, *Taking a Nap* (June 17, 1871: p. 569), an incident on the train journey from Chicago to Council Bluffs. Both men may have agreed to share the expense of hiring Cody, although it is likely that Flynn paid.

America of 1870 was even more of a hunter's paradise than it is today, and teemed with every variety of wild life. On the plains were huge herds of buffalo; in the mountains hunters could stalk big game such as wapiti and elk, as well as bear, bighorn sheep and deer. In the forests there were hordes of wild turkeys. Moreover, the lone English traveller would seldom be without an invitation from a friendly civilian or army officer to join a hunting party.[2] Such invitations were usually extended in the convivial ambience of the Pullman car or hotel bar after the first round, if not by a letter of introduction to the commander of an army post.

Houghton arrived at the frontier itself late in January. Omaha, the starting point of his western travels, was 'a wonderful mushrooming town whose growth was almost visibly apparent'. Snow lay everywhere; but from inside the warmth of his Pullman car, waiting to leave the Union Pacific station, he found one of his most sympathetic subjects. He looked out on to the park between Farnham and Jones Streets, to see children whizzing down a slope on sleds. Thinking no doubt of his own children, he made a sketch for *Coasting at Omaha* (January 19, 1871: p. 31), a lyrical and nostalgic scene of boys and girls sledding in the crisp snow.

How had the noble savage deteriorated into the appalling state of physical and moral depravity which Houghton had seen at Niagara Falls? Now he was out West, he was anxious to visit the more independent tribes and gain a deeper insight into the Indian 'problem'. West of Omaha he stopped off at Clarks in Merrick County, Nebraska, and reported to the nearby army post at North Loup, to arrange for a stay of several days at the Pawnee Agency, then located in the fork of the Loup River near Genoa.

The Pawnee were not the best example of the un-

Shooting Turkeys in an American Forest 1869. Engraved by W. Measoms. 12 × 9. *Graphic*, December 23, 1871. From left to right the hunters are: the artist (in fur hat), Alonzo Slafter, William Slafter, and the innkeeper, John McPherson.

Pawnees Gambling. 1870
Engraved by Swain.
Graphic, July 23, 1870.

tamed Indian of the Plains. They lived in peace by col-
laborating with their conquerors against the hostile
tribes of the region. The celebrated Pawnee Battalion of
1866–7 helped to protect the builders of the Union
Pacific Line, and the tribe continued to provide scouts
and mercenaries for the cavalry regiments stationed in
eastern Nebraska. In turn, they received protection from
their old enemy, the still active Sioux. The Pawnee were
both farmers and hunters, and at the time of Houghton's

pilgrimage, lived a traditional if somewhat debauched
life, in and around picturesque villages of earth lodges.
At a time when the Western Army was fighting Indians
on and off throughout the West and in dire need of
allies, the Pawnee were a favoured tribe and their village
something of a showpiece for foreign visitors.

With Cooper and Longfellow in mind, Houghton recalled the early contact of the white man with the Indian;
for all the good that contact had done, it would have been

Pawnee Squaws 1870. Wood engraving. *Graphic*, February 22, 1873.

The Return of Hiawatha 1871.
Watercolour on board. 30 × 42.
Victoria & Albert Museum,
London.
The title suggests Longfellow's
poem, but Houghton interpreted
the subject in a very different
way showing the lovers struggle
for survival.

better if it had never taken place. The Indian possessed a marvellous aptitude for catching and clinging to the vices of his unwelcome white neighbours, while ignoring the virtues. One of these was the unexpected habit of cursing and swearing on every occasion, 'as if it were a keen luxury newly discovered, a fresh language learned'.

But the Indian's greatest vice was, of course, drinking. Although 'firewater' was appreciated by Cooper's noble savage, Houghton discovered that the modern Hiawatha loved to drink even more! He commented:

However they came by it, they were soon drawn to it as a moth to the candle-light; and now, whatever Indian by any odd chance gets involved in a city or village of the whites is almost certain to be champion drunkard of the place. Government, in past times, has not disdained to ply them with whisky, and has been able to obtain from them in return, substantial concessions, a disgraceful practice which in these latter more enlightened times has happily been abandoned, but abandoned too late to save the poor savage race from the evils of intoxication and moral ruin.

The Pawnee also loved to gamble; inside or outside their lodges, it didn't matter. Their favourite card-games, like those of white gamblers, were seven-up, high-low-jack, whist and euchre.

Moreover, the Indian squaw shared her man's vices to the full; she was, in fact, but a shade less masculine than her Hiawatha. She not only drank as much as her lords, but gambled even more. The beauty of Longfellow's heroine, Minnehaha, was found to be more myth than reality. In the full-page illustration *Hiawatha and Minnehaha* (July 16, 1870: p. 60), Houghton depicts Minnehaha as a young squaw carrying a large bundle of firewood with the dogged resignation of a 'hopeless slave', while Hiawatha, her haughty master, follows behind smoking his calumet in deep meditation. As far as the Pawnee was concerned, thought Houghton, the modern traveller must search long before he hears the musical laughter of Minnehaha and other coppery belles of the forest. Yet industrious as the squaws were, they also had the daunting task of trading the fruits of their skill. It was here that they were taken advantage of and exploited unmercifully, because unfortunately for them, they were not equal to the cunning of the frontier trader.

> The women will work hard month after month at making the gorgeous buffalo robes which one sees in the winter seasons, adorning the sleighs on the fashionable course of eastern cities. . . . For those gorgeous robes which sell in the east at high prices, the squaws receive a pittance of brown sugar or molasses. This is of the poorest quality, and seems to be sand with a soaking of treacle. But the full iniquity of the hard bargain does not stop there. When the grasping trader measures out his thickened treacle, according to frontier commercial usage when dealing with the Indians, he thrusts his three fingers in the shallow cup, and only gives out what little substance finds room in the small space not already so basely occupied.

Little wonder, Houghton reflected, that the Indians looked with contempt on the white man and his ways.

Yet he did find something remaining of the uncorrupted savage when watching Indian boys playing the

Bartering with Indians 1870. Wood engraving. 11¾ × 8½. *Graphic*, March 11, 1871.

Pawnee Boys Playing Hoop and Pole 1870.
Wood engraving.
$7\frac{7}{8} \times 8\frac{7}{8}$.
Published as *North American Indian Sports*.
Graphic, March 4, 1871.

popular Pawnee hoop and pole game. He depicted the scene, entitled *North American Indian Sports* (March 4, 1871: p. 204), with an obvious sympathy for the players. The game itself was usually played on smooth ground with a small hoop or ring, and poles or sticks four feet long. The aim was to dart the point of the stick directly through the hoop and catch it on the two prongs at the heel. One of the players rolls the hoop in front of the

others, and each tries to dart his stick through the moving circle. Sport, the artist quickly observed, played a vital role in Indian life:

Those who have witnessed the Indians engaged in their forest and field sports, bear unanimous evidence of their marvellous prowess, their exceeding skill, and their tiger-like savage valour. The Indian braves the hideous-eyed and monster-headed buffalo, as the

[96]

English gentleman does deer or fox, entangles him in nets, and drags him earthward; leaps to his side and plunges the long knife deep into his thickly-coated side; and mocks at the panther and bear as game unworthy of his pains. Such strength and courage, such tenacity of purpose and grim bravery in will and action, the Indian learns in childhood and youth.

Before he left the reservation and returned to Clarks,

Houghton was unexpectedly honoured with a farewell feast by Chief Crooked Hand. He returned the compliment by illustrating the event in a convivial full page scene, entitled *A Smoke with Friendlies* (November 4, 1871: p. 445), in which he depicted himself with Flynn seated by an open fire, smoking the pipe of peace. Game was cooked, Indian fashion, over an open fire, and when it was eaten, squaws moved around liberally dispensing

A Smoke with Friendlies 1870. Wood engraving. $8\frac{7}{8} \times 11\frac{7}{8}$. *Graphic*, November 4, 1871.

Carrying the Mail 1870. Wood engraving. *Graphic*, July 29, 1871.

'firewater'. The Indian, he discovered, was much more sophisticated than he appeared to be on first acquaintance. Socially he was as amusing a dinner host as it was possible to meet anywhere.

His oddities convulse you with laughter; his powers of imitation are inexhaustible; his mimicries are full of a potent satire which unconscious simplicity alone can wield.

Warmed by the spirited and unconventional quality of the evening, the Bohemian in Houghton concluded that there was a 'perpetual poetry' in the Indian way of life. He could well imagine all present to be the descendants of those dashing heroes of the woods and rivers whom Cooper had immortalized, somewhat tamed and civilized, but still irrepressible. Compared to the prosaic reality of these modern days, theirs was a life, he thought, which emphasized living instead of getting. As such it was poetry indeed, highly romantic, and so worthy of the eloquence of the greatest bards.

As he travelled further into the land of sky and grass, Houghton became increasingly aware of the vastness of the Great Plains. It was as if they had been made as a playground for long-striding giants, rather than for mere mankind. So *much* space stretched emptily from one horizon to another that it looked more like the sea than the earth! How could he ever communicate this to those who lived in densely-populated England: how convey the effect of the prairies on which, although flat for miles and miles, men could get lost, or die of starvation, and whose wavy monotony was only broken by the wide and perfect circle of the horizon? Yet there was much to see. Since the end of the Civil War, Americans had been trekking westward; many to fall victim to the Indians, desperadoes, or the fraudulent schemes of their compatriots. After the Pacific Railroad had been completed, hundreds of thousands of emigrants had joined them.

Many of the newcomers were a tough breed of farmers, but even so, pioneer experience was harsh; the odds against taming and cultivating the plains seemed overwhelming. In spite of the fact that the Indians were being

subdued, in spite of the fact that the land was fertile and crops needed less than the usual care, a farm on the plains of Nebraska was a place of never-ending toil and struggle. Houghton rightly guessed that much of the pioneers' hope and belief in the future depended on contact with family and the outside world. As he watched the difficulties of conveying mail across the swollen Platte River near Fort McPherson, he saw how tenuous the settlers' links with the outside world were. Their contact with 'The States', as they called the East, or the Old Country (usually England, Scotland, Sweden or Germany); the memories of childhood or an old life; these were precariously sustained, if at all, by the trickle of mail that took weeks and sometimes months for delivery. So far, the railroad hadn't changed that.

A Scallawag 1870.
Wood engraving.
Graphic, July 8, 1871.

VIII: The Buffalo Hunters

Houghton had looked forward to taking part in a buffalo hunt with boyish enthusiasm. If America was more than a country and a people, if it was an idea of freedom, then buffalo hunting stood for the adventure he would hope to find there.

He could not have timed it better. At the close of the Civil War it was estimated that there were some fifteen million buffalo grazing the prairies. By 1885 fewer than a thousand remained alive. One of the most colourful chapters of the history of the West was about to come to an abrupt end. Bereft of both the nomadic Indian tribes, and the buffalo they lived upon, the vast treeless prairies would become the wheatbelt of Nebraska: the western fringe of what is now Middle America.

It was the coming of the railroad which finally sealed the fate of the great herds, when the Union Pacific and Kansas Pacific laid their tracks westward. Even before the first trains chugged west from Omaha, thousands of buffalo were shot to supply meat for the construction gangs building the Union Pacific and Kansas Pacific lines. After completion, colonization agents promoted package tours and hunts along with settlement, while the publicity men planted stories of the great sport and of the small fortunes the professional hide hunters were making. Passengers aboard trains were encouraged to join in the fun and pick off stragglers with carbines and pistols.

Such slaughter paled beside the systematic butchery practised by squads of professional hide hunters intent on making a fortune from the buffalo hides so much in demand back East and in England. Among them were men like Wild Bill Hickok, Charley Reynolds and others, who had no use for the meat and left the carcasses to stink and rot. One year after Houghton's visit the sheds of every railroad station on the plains were crammed from floor to ceiling with hides. The whitened bones

In Search of Buffalo 1870. Wood engraving. *Graphic*, January 14, 1871.

were piled in wagons, and ground down into fertilizer. Mari Sandoz tells us in her sardonic epic, *The Buffalo Hunters* (1954) that the business 'paid for the railroads, drove the Indians back, helped bring rapid settlement, (and) turned money loose locally'.

Shortly after the joining of the Union Pacific and Central Pacific lines on May 10, 1869, Wild Bill Hickok was hired by Senator Wilson of Massachusetts to guide a large party of 'dudes', as the locals dubbed them. They were on safari five weeks with tents, valets and maids. Wild Bill was in demand for a while, but after a barroom gunfight with troopers of the Seventh Cavalry, in which several were killed, he retired hastily from the field, leaving it open to the greatest of them all, Buffalo Bill Cody. Houghton's daughter Cecily is quoted by Sullivan as saying that it was Buffalo Bill who took her father buffalo hunting.

At the time Cody had yet to achieve the fame that was to change his whole way of life. E. Z. C. Judson, or as he was better known, 'Ned Buntline', the dime Western writer, had made him famous overnight in his serial 'Buffalo Bill, King of the Border Men'.[1] Cody, however, still worked for the army as chief of scouts attached to the Fifth Cavalry, stationed at Fort McPherson. But even a chief scout's wages didn't go far for a man of his flamboyant tastes. So during the long intervals between campaigning against hostile Indians, Cody devoted more and more of his time to organizing private hunting parties for wealthy bigwigs, prominent politicians, and foreign notables.

Cody was twenty-four years old and strikingly handsome. The scout stood six feet tall, with long light brown hair cascading in ringlets over his broad, buckskinned shoulders. His quick-searching eyes missed nothing as they gazed out from under the shade of a wide-brimmed felt hat. Cody took the artist to Fort McPherson, a large cavalry post in the forks of the Platte River, a ride of some fourteen miles to the east.[2]

Houghton must have delighted in his convivial personality, so much like his own. He wrote of Cody's companions that they were

Indian-like in their thin, high cheekedboned, swarthy, long-haired, hard-featured physiognomies, as if contact with Indians, and participation in their mode of life, had twisted them into a personal likeness.

They were also like himself: each day was lived to the full as if it might be the last! Indeed, they were haunted by the idea that they would die a sudden and violent death. Many – veterans of the Civil War – had been outlaws. Some of them still were. Living among Indians who might at any time turn hostile, frozen by bitterly cold winters, and scorched by the summer's intense heat, they lived in a constant state of tension and anxiety. Houghton revelled in their swashbuckling comradeship and thought them 'real Westerners all right, the Don Quixotes of the great plains of America'.

The favourite locale of Buffalo Bill's hunting parties was then the tall-grass country between the Platte and Republican Rivers, which abounded in game, particularly buffalo. Hunting was usually done under the patronage of the army, whose job it was to patrol and guard the frontier. Special Order No. 19, dated February 15, 1870, issued by headquarters at Fort McPherson, authorized Brevet Lieutenant-Colonel Campbell Dallas Emory, Captain of the Ninth Infantry, to command a mixed unit of the Ninth and Fifth Cavalry on a hunting expedition,[3] which probably took place along Medicine and Red Willow Creeks.

Besides Houghton and Flynn,[4] the party included several hide hunters and some friendly Indians to act as scouts and guides. There was Charley Reynolds and California Joe; Helen Cody Westmore,[5] Cody's sister, went along too, as did Dr Frank Powell, an Omaha journalist, and Major W. H. Brown, a well-known cavalry officer who first introduced Cody to Ned Buntline, and who was subsequently immortalized himself in a dime Western. Houghton and his companions dressed themselves in individual variations of Western hunting gear; all carried hunting rifles, and most side arms. Houghton himself sported a pair of heavy revolvers

stuck into Mexican holsters on a broad gunbelt. He described the preparations:

It is as if you were making a journey into a far land. Men must go in a large company; and besides a few might be overcome, robbed, slain, scalped by hostile Indian tribes. Provisions of the least perishable and the homeliest sort are carefully packed, enough to last and for contingencies. The luxuries are confined to the rawest of Bourbon whisky, and the blackest of Virginia tobacco.

Finally the wagons were ready and the party set out, 'rifles are slung across shoulders, powder flasks and shot pouches bumping this side and that'. Horses snorted and reared as they galloped forward.

Houghton, carried away with the 'limpid clearness' of the landscape, and 'intoxicating crispness' of the air, continued:

The train winds out of the inhabited places, and

stretches over the grassy and shrubby plains; the hamlets become less and less frequent; the wheatfields and mining stations disappear one after another; nature resumes in the wilderness its virgin majesty, and you are at last out among the trackless hills and strange solitudes, experiencing a sensation wholly new. Now and then, the light smoke curls up from behind a distant hill, or a bedizened figure appears on its side, betraying the whereabouts of an Indian camp; the Indians who are guiding your expedition tell you that these are Choctaws, Ute, or Sioux. Perhaps the hunting party stops at the encampment, and the skillful in the Indian tongue put the squatter settlement through a cross-examination as to whether they have seen any buffaloes.

As the party entered deep canyons of the high plains country, the going became difficult. He depicted the scene in *Crossing a Canyon* (July 29, 1871: p. 117), and wrote:

There are deep gulleys, whose sides are too steep for

the horses and oxen to draw the wagons down; and to get over them, it is necessary to make pulleys out of the humanity present, and to haul the wagons up, or let them down, by means of strong ropes. All hands 'turn to' and likely enough, the hands which you brought kid-gloved and sleekly soft from Pall Mall club and West End drawing room, will be drafted into service now. Meanwhile, one of the chiefs of the expedition sits aloft on a neighbouring ledge, overlooking the difficult operations below, now and then shouting out – 'A little tighter, you there! Jake, give him more rope – slack down you coons, slack down!'

The party then entered the habitat of the Republican River herd and camped on Red Willow Creek. The following morning, all hands mounted and met at the starting-point of the hunt. It was not long before the hunters spotted their first buffalo, standing on the crest of a hill. Houghton's pulse beat faster:

There stands the monster, stock still, with the strong steady majestic gaze of his tribe. He is the forerunner,

The First Buffalo 1870. Wood engraving. $5\frac{7}{8} \times 8\frac{7}{8}$. *Graphic*, July 29, 1871.

Crossing a Canyon 1870. Wood engraving. $9\frac{7}{8} \times 8\frac{7}{8}$. *Graphic*, July 29, 1871. (facing page)

outpost, picket of his particular herd, browsing and keeping guard on the frontier of their domain. A great, tough-ribbed, hard and hairy-headed, and bearded bull, he is one of that outer circle of buffaloes who is always found around the cows and young. He watches for two enemies, for the Kiota wolf, a cruel and rapacious beast which stealthily pounces upon their young, their feeble or their wounded; and for man, in the shape of the Indian, who vie with the Kiota in their cunning and their greed.

The buffalo, he thought, seemed to feel at the outset that there was to be deadly sport, and braced himself to face it. He never declined a contest but always accepted it with 'noble fury'. At the start of the chase Houghton wondered whether it was on the part of the man or the buffalo, as the hunters were led on at full tilt. Rifles began to crackle and he could not help but admire the impetuous courage of the beast, the 'lordly stubbornness', the 'ferocious pride of his carriage', and the 'warlike significance of every motion'. The artist felt there was no other scene which more vividly contrasted the ingenuity of man and the physical prowess of animals: 'Were it not for weapons which brain has put into the hands of men – weapons moral and physical – there could not be a moment's conflict'. The day's hunting closed with convivial gatherings by flickering campfires. He depicted such a scene in one of his finest illustrations, *Camping Out* (August 5, 1871: p. 136).

There was constant danger of attack by Indians. Roving bands of fiercely hostile Sioux were never far away. A lookout had to be kept at all times to prevent a swift and murderous assault on the camp. Young Sioux braves, militantly opposed to any intrusion of their hunting grounds, and the indiscriminate slaughter of game, had the habit of taking matters into their own hands. On one occasion Houghton rode out with Cody and made a sketch which he later elaborated as *On the Scout* (March 9, 1872: p. 220), a rare portrayal of the celebrated plainsman as a young man.

Camping Out 1870. Wood engraving. $8\frac{7}{8} \times 8\frac{7}{8}$. *Graphic*, August 5, 1871. (facing page)

Studies of Buffalo Heads for *Camping Out* 1870. Pencil. From the artist's sketchbook in the Print Room, Victoria & Albert Museum, London.

On the Scout 1870. Wood engraving. $8\frac{7}{8} \times 8\frac{7}{8}$. *Graphic*, March 9, 1872.

A Jamboree 1870.
Wood engraving.
12 × 9.
Graphic, September 23, 1871.

The party had been away for three days, and had covered some ninety miles, by the time the hunters returned to make camp in a grove of cottonwoods close to Fort McPherson by the Platte River. Here, on the eve of the artist's departure for Salt Lake City, a pow-wow, or campfire celebration, wound up the hunt. It was a Rabelaisian affair. Cody, who knew how to put on a show, arranged horse races in which his two best mounts, Tall Bull and Powder Face, were the winners. There were Indian dances too, and Houghton was challenged to a drinking contest by a friendly Indian chief (probably Spotted Tail, the cosmopolitan Brulé chief who found it difficult to resist joining in such parties). Artist and chief were still in the running, even when Cody's supply of whisky ran out. The contest then continued with brandy, and Houghton was finally the winner on points because the chief had to retire on the verge of bursting. In the animated *Buffalo-Hunting – A Jamboree* (September 23, 1871: p. 300), Houghton depicts the festive party dancing to the improvised accompaniment of a cooking-pot drum, beaten by the stock of a revolver.

On February 18, at North Platte, he boarded a westbound train that would carry him on to Salt Lake City, the promised land of the Mormons. New vistas took the place of the rolling sandhills and the level valley of the Platte. Beyond Cheyenne the ascent of the Rocky Mountains began, and the railroad climbed rugged granite hills, winding in and out of interminable snowsheds. After Laramie came the high plains, followed by a region of arid valleys, abounding in fantastic vividly coloured buttes and pinnacles, and wide windy canyons. Then the track crawled around the spurs of the Uintah Mountains, finally to cross the dividing ridge of the continent. Utah territory was entered west of Wahsatch, a region of extraordinary and strange beauty. Houghton was overwhelmed by the splendour of the landscape. The train went through Devil's Gap, and then:

> we reach Ogden, the junction of the main Pacific road with the branch line, which swings off here to Salt Lake City. It is on the edge of the valley, and from thence you may look off upon the vast domain and smiling landscape, and exclaim to yourself that it is no wonder the Mormons selected such a spot for their retreat.

[107]

The Mormons were considered a problem in America, and their polygamy was deplored. From the very beginning, the movement had known persecution and massacre; but since the murder of the Mormon founding father, Joseph Smith, in 1844, the sect had flourished beyond the wildest expectations. In 1847 Brigham Young organized and led the settlement into the promised land, the Great Salt Lake Valley. Here the Mormons prospered. Strong in faith and purpose, they ploughed and planted, dug irrigation channels, built houses and founded towns.

The Times, which gave the Mormons some much-needed publicity during the period of the Chartist movement (1848-55), remarked in 1855 that 'its combination

Mormon Family on their way to Salt Lake City 1870. Wood engraving. 9 × 9. *Graphic*, November 4, 1871.

of Judaism, Mohammedanism, socialism, despotism, and the grossest superstition, with much practical good sense, combine to make it the most singular phenomenon of modern times'. By 1860, more than 200,000 Mormon settlers were rapidly developing the Kingdom of God in the Wilderness, the future state of Utah.

It was a success story of great interest to Houghton, especially as the majority of settlers had been recruited from the poor and downtrodden of Britain. He arrived in Salt Lake City on February 19, and stayed at the Walker House Hotel. During a three-day visit, he seems to have seen everything of importance; he visited the Mormon theatre; he talked to Mormons and Gentiles; he interviewed Brigham Young; and attended a Mormon service in the Great Tabernacle. 'The American "Turks"' he found, 'big, raw-boned-looking men, with goat tufts on their chins; their women, for the most part, very sorrowful and haggard-looking'. Brigham Young's complex of residences he thought 'harem-like', the grounds being surrounded by a high stone wall, and the artist escorted by two 'sentinels'. Young's office was in a little building connected with the principal residence (The Lion House) by a covered passage-way.

The Grand Turk of Utah himself greatly impressed the artist. Brigham Young was no ordinary person, but:
> . . . a broad-shouldered, muscular man, nearly three-score and ten, with thin reddish gray hair, and fore-head large and much wrinkled, light in complexion, his mouth set in a determined way, and a keen, cold, cruel, blue eye; his whole manner and appearance be-tokening inflexibility of will, shrewdness, and cunning.

Young talked freely on the subject of polygamy and his commonwealth, entering 'easily into argument upon that or any other point you chose to broach'. He invited the artist to attend his sermon the following day. So, Houghton spent the afternoon of Sunday, February 20, in the huge, egg-shaped tabernacle on Main Street, listening to the immense organ and a sermon by his 'magnetic' host. From this experience he created the finest of his Mormon scenes, a masterly double-page depicting the administration of the Sacrament, entitled *Service in the Mormon Tabernacle, Salt Lake City* (September 2, 1871: pp. 228-9). The similarity of theme

Service in the Mormon Tabernacle, Salt Lake City 1870. Wood engraving. $11\frac{3}{4} \times 19\frac{3}{4}$. *Graphic*, September 2, 1871.

prompts a comparison with the Shaker illustration, *Shaker Evans at Home*, in which the Shaker leader is also depicted preaching extempore. The scene in the Mormon tabernacle, however, provides a fascinating close-up of the diverse characters at the heart of this extraordinary mass movement which so largely helped make the modern West. By contrast, the tranquil, almost

attitude towards Mormonism maintained by Liberals and Radicals, notably Dickens and Burton, influenced the artist. He himself was only too aware of what the British converts were escaping from. One sees in his scenes of Mormon life, therefore, something of a note of respect.

Only once does Houghton poke fun, in his gently

complacent Shaker audience seems to belong more to colonial times.

Apart from their richly pictorial quality, Houghton's Mormon illustrations have the added strength of revealing his personal compassion for humbler people. In them one feels him to be examining and questioning. After Susan's death, he searched continually for some ideal way of life, usually experienced by simple and ordinary people. How do you live? Are you *content?* Confronted by an 'ideal' state, his questioning becomes more fervent. Very obviously, too, the sympathetic

humorous *The Bishop and the Gentile* (August 5, 1871: p. 672); a comment on the growing challenge to Mormon custom. An old Mormon bishop is out for a walk with his wives, the youngest of whom is seen coyly responding to the courtly overtures of a handsome young Gentile, or non-believer.

Perhaps the Mormon Zion was the closest to being the Common Man's Utopia which he had hoped to find in America. With the Mormon illustrations, 'Graphic America' came to an end. Despite the editorial announcement that there would also be scenes of life and character

Cornered 1870. Wood engraving. *Graphic*, July 8, 1871.

The Bishop and the Gentile 1870. Wood engraving. $8\frac{7}{8} \times 8\frac{7}{8}$. *Graphic*, August 5, 1871. (facing page)

in California and the Southern States, none were ever published. A hastily scribbled note in the artist's sketch-book does, however, indicate that he may have continued his transcontinental journey as far as San Francisco.[6] More than likely, Thomas cabled him there, requesting an early return to England. Momentous events in Europe had first claim on his time.

He was back in New York by the middle of March. There he completed his woodblocks and took them to Franklin Square to show Charles Parsons.[7] When they appeared, American reaction to the Western illustra-tions was much more favourable than it had been to the New York illustrations. Pictures of the West were then as much a novelty in New York and Boston as they were in London, and they were republished freely.

East and West, America stimulated Houghton into making his most uncompromising venture. 'Graphic America' represents a great and unusual achievement. No other artist had been given, or would be given again, the freedom to describe as well as to depict his impres-sions of such an important theme. By 1879 the exuberant chauvinism of Imperialism had completely transformed the magazine media. Artists, if they were involved with the *Graphic* or the *Illustrated London News* at all, were given the title of Special Artist, and packed off as pic-torial journalists to scribble on-the-spot sketches of wars for Empire which others completed and developed as 'death-or-glory' illustrations. Only in the present cen-tury did the creative artist return to the pages of the mass-circulation periodical as a free-wheeling social commentator.

IX: The Light That Failed

The autocratic regime of Napoleon III was openly on the defensive, and controlling with difficulty the mounting popular disenchantment with the Second Empire. Rochefort's insurrection of January 1870 was a taste of what was to come. France was moving towards war with Germany, as well as a confrontation with her own revolutionaries. Thomas wanted his most experienced Special Artist for what was obviously to be the arena of his next assignment. Houghton had been back in London since the end of April. In America he had been homesick for some time, and returning to his beloved London and his customary way of life made him feel at peace with the world. It was good indeed to be back in his own studio,[1] his own house, and after the loneliness of constant travel, to resume contact with his children, his parents and his friends.

But the return to the comfort and domesticity of family life proved to be of short duration. In July 1870 war broke out between France and Germany. Thomas summoned Houghton to his office in the Strand. Here was the *Graphic*'s biggest opportunity to establish itself. A good war sold more copies of a picture paper than any other event. One had broken out within eight months of publication!

Houghton arrived in Paris during the early days of August 1870. The city was gay and diverting. The fashionable cafés were crowded and the war seemed far away. But as fond as he was of the social life, he had much to do. Thomas feared that the *Illustrated London News* would leave the *Graphic* a long way behind with its team of six artists in the field; a team which included the doyen of Special Artists, William Simpson (1823-99). Somehow Thomas had to ensure that the *Graphic*, with only three artists, would equal, if not excel, the coverage of its older rival.[2] Houghton helped to solve the problem by contributing some of the most dramatic illustrations published of the Franco-Prussian War and its aftermath, the Commune. Yet one can well imagine that Houghton found himself overwhelmed and sometimes at a complete loss. During his years as an illustrator, he had always tried to avoid news events, and he remained reluctant, even as the drama began to unfold, to visualize it in any other but the most eloquently artistic terms.

The war, he found, was not going well for the French; their armies, wretchedly equipped and badly led, suffered one defeat after another, culminating on September 2, 1870, with the disaster of Sedan, where 100,000 men including Napoleon III himself were taken prisoner. On September 4 the Republic was proclaimed and a provisional government of National Defence was formed by the ageing Adolphe Thiers. For a time, Leon Gambetta, Minister of the Interior, strove to re-organize French resistance, but it was a hopeless task. By September 19 the Prussians had Paris completely surrounded, cut off from the rest of the country and preparing for a long siege.

The Siege of Paris had settled into an extraordinary routine. Parisians made light of their ordeal, and took Sunday walks to inspect the big guns and the fortifications. There were daily military parades, and nightly bombardments were watched almost like firework displays. Citizens ate horse, cat and even rat flesh, saturated in characteristically delectable sauces. The painters de Neuville and Detaille built themselves a huge high platform overlooking the city and systematically depicted the ordeal of the French capital; while Nadar's gas-filled balloons sailed into the night skies carrying mail (including drawings) and passengers over the German lines. Less established artists like Doré, Degas and Manet served in the National Guard, brooding about the uncertain future as they performed their sometimes ludicrous duties. Then a bitterly cold winter set in to intensify the sufferings of hunger, although for those with money to burn, a thriving black market could supply every luxury. There was no work. Revolutionary organizations began to extend their influence through workshops and soup kitchens. The hope that Gambetta and the new armies would eventually triumph began to fade. Divided by increasing dissension, Paris finally capitulated to the Prussians on January 28, 1871. Less than two months later, it was to experience the even greater trauma of civil war.

Republican Paris blamed the monarchists for the victory march of 30,000 German troops through the city. Parisians scrubbed streets to erase their shame. The Conservative government of Thiers now moved to control the increasingly rebellious capital. The pay of the National Guard was abolished, and an attempt made to strip them of their guns. When the move failed, Thiers fled to Versailles. The Central Committee of the Commune quickly established itself. On March 26, inspired by the Paris Commune of 1793, a new municipal council voted to form the historic Commune of 1871.

The goals of the Commune were moderate enough: it wanted what the working people had wanted for years – better wages and working conditions, plus municipal reform – but to the National Assembly, the rebels were dangerous revolutionaries to be put down whatever the cost. Reaction, or rather over-reaction, was both dramatic and immediate. Bismarck, alarmed by the gathering storm which could easily spread east to Germany, promptly released 60,000 of the 400,000 French regulars held prisoner of war. They were sent by train to be re-mobilized to crush the Commune.

At first the Commune seemed invulnerable, but with so many different factions it soon became hopelessly divided. Finally, on May 21, Thiers and his generals launched their counter-offensive. In seven days the Commune was overthrown, and thousands of Communards and suspected sympathizers killed in ferocious reprisals. It was officially acknowledged that 100,000 died or were taken prisoner during the struggle. France would not forget that week, the most violent in the history of the nation.

Houghton would not forget it either. The war – and particularly the aftermath of the Paris Commune – was

A Barricade in Paris 1871. Engraved by H. Harral. $8\frac{7}{8} \times 11\frac{7}{8}$. *Graphic*, April 8, 1871. Houghton captures the spirit of revolt in a scene which took place at the junction of the Rue des Martyrs and Boulevard Rochechouart, following General Vinoy's ill-fated attempt to carry off the guns of Montmartre on March 18, 1871.

a turning point for both his art and his ideas. He had witnessed a bloodbath caused by the most desperate class conflict, and the Commune inevitably became something of a test of his own dissent. His response was to recoil at the unrestricted barbarity of the reality, to the point of becoming nonpartisan.

He produced a chronicle terrible in its fidelity to the truth. He began in his usual manner, depicting significant aspects of everyday incidents during the Siege and the early days of the Commune. But then, as the Versaillais smashed their way into Paris, Houghton turned from genre towards a drama-charged reporting of history. While complying with his duties as a Special Artist, he expressed his true feelings in illustrations unique among his work as a social commentator.

The Commune series followed an earlier group of illustrations devoted to various scenes before and after the Siege The first, entitled *The Raid on the Useless Mouths* (September 17, 1870: p. 274), appeared with a short text by the artist. Paris, Houghton wrote, was obsessively arresting those thought hostile to the national interest, those who were making ready for an extension of business when the able-bodied had shouldered arms and joined the ranks.

Artists could very easily qualify for such summary justice, and were frequently hurried off to jail, if only for being suspected of being suspicious. Because of their habit of scribbling sketches in pocket notebooks, they were inevitably thought to be Prussian spies. The French artist René Morin was mobbed and made prisoner after being discovered sketching by irate patriotic citizens. The risk of being seen drawing or found with drawings became so acute that artists had to resort to subterfuge. Few were as ingenious as Simpson, who made his sketches in a book of cigarette papers, so that in the event of being apprehended, he could make a cigarette of the sketch, or chew it before the eyes of his captors. Houghton, who possessed the enviable faculty of remembering what he saw, escaped such suspicion. But his turn was to come later, during the Commune, when a woman soldier, discovering him taking notes at a meeting, proposed drenching him in petrol and setting him on fire for being, as she thought, a Versaillais spy. 'To cut matters short', Houghton wrote, 'I told her I was only a

[114]

newspaper correspondent, and she did not interfere any further, especially as I contributed two sous towards expenses'.

On March 18 came the event that was to light the torch of revolution in Paris; Vinoy's ill-starred attempt to carry off the cannon of Montmartre. Houghton hastened at once to the scene and witnessed the astonishing spectacle of popular exaltation; detachments of regular troops fraternizing everywhere with revolutionary workers and the National Guard, while men, women and

urchins pulled up paving stones and dragged furniture out of shops to build a vast barricade. He captured all the spirit of the occasion in a lively full-page woodblock entitled *A Barricade in Paris* (April 8, 1871: p. 312).

The Commune was the master of Paris for two months; then, on Sunday, May 21, the Versaillais army suddenly began their invasion of the city at three in the afternoon. Parisians did not learn the news until the Monday morning. Houghton, who had spent that Sunday with friends at La Varenne St Hilaire, south-west of Paris, returned by the last train and had just got into his bed. In a letter to the *Graphic* he wrote, 'I was suddenly startled from sleep by a band of Federals (Communards) passing rapidly down the street, and shortly afterwards, drums were beating the *rappel*, clarions sounding the *générale* and the bells of the neighbouring churches pealing forth the ominous warning of the tocsin. All thought of sleep was out of the question, so dressing hastily, I went out to gather some information. By this time it was six o'clock, groups were forming at street corners, a peasant was saying that he had been to the Northern station (Gare du Nord), where he had been turned back, and the Prussians had cut the lines. A baker, coming up, said, "Do you know the news? They're in – came in last night"'.[3]

As the city awakened, the streets began to bristle with barricades. The entire population was put to work reinforcing or building new ones. Everyone who passed by was forced to lend a hand. Simpson, venturing outside his hotel in the Rue Caumartin, was challenged by a Commune soldier and ordered to work at a barricade. Women were to be seen everywhere, 'women in rags, and women in silk dresses', adds Edith Thomas in her book on women during the Commune, *The Women Incendiaries*. 'Young girls and old ladies were sewing and filling sandbags, were working with pickaxes and mattocks, all day and, by gaslight, all night'. As the Versaillais advanced, women – they were called *Vengereuses* – fought shoulder to shoulder with their men. 'Mostly unorganized', writes Thomas, 'they had come there either because their husband or lover was involved in the battle, or because a barricade had been built at the end of their street'. After witnessing such scenes, Houghton devoted himself to depicting what to him appeared to be the

Paris Under the Commune: Women's Club at the Boule Noire, Boulevard Rochechouart 1871. Engraved by H. Harral. $8\frac{7}{8} \times 11\frac{3}{4}$. Graphic, June 3, 1871.

'*The Commune or Death*' –
Women of Montmartre 1871.
Wood engraving.
$11\frac{7}{8} \times 8\frac{7}{8}$.
Graphic, June 10, 1871.

Commune's most significant feature: the large numbers of women actively involved.

The Women's Clubs, which had exerted great influence during the Siege, had regained all their importance. Houghton ventured into one of them, the famous La Boule Noire, in which the female patriots held their meetings. The speakers sat around the edge of the platform wearing very homely cotton dresses and white linen caps, offset by a large red scarf around their waists and a red rosette on the bosom. One of the speakers appealed to the women present to defend the barricades to death, exposing to public shame the men who were hiding in their own homes, or worse still, had fled from the city, hidden in furniture vans. Houghton depicted the occasion in *The Women's Club at the Boule Noire, Boulevard Rochechouart* (June 3, 1871: p. 521).

During the night he saw a battalion of women marching by, large red flags flapping at their head, to defend a barricade in Montmartre. Against the background of the Hotel de Ville in flames, it was an extraordinary and vivid spectacle. 'Each', he wrote, 'had a *chassepot* rifle slung over her shoulders, and a belt and cartouche box, amply supplied with cartridges round her waist'. Who they were he did not know. 'I fancied', he added, 'I recognized at the head of the company one of the favourite orators of the club at the Boule Noire, who seemed to take the place of an officer'. This column, we now know, was the entire committee of the *Union des Femmes*, headed by the celebrated women's leader, the militant Nathalie Lemel, who, on the orders of the Commune, marched out to defend Les Batignolles.[4] In his illustration *The Commune or Death* (June 10, 1871: p. 541) Houghton evoked all the savage bitterness which motivated these women and their superhuman determination to fight for what they believed was right.

The violence and blackness of these illustrations is unusual for Houghton. He shows the actual, but only in so far as it is significant. Where he distorts or emphasizes, it is for the purpose of embracing the essence of the reality that confronted him. Nothing could characterize the struggle between a well-disciplined army and a 'rabble' of determined women more strikingly than his device of giving a semblance of disordered mobility to the women's battalion against a background of Paris in flames. Nor could anything indicate more clearly the ambivalence of Houghton's sympathies.

That he did not forget the social is shown by the individual character of each participant, for the five figures leading the battalion included most of the inner leadership of the *Union des Femmes*: besides Nathalie Lemel, bookbinder, there is Marie Leloup, seamstress, and Elizabeth Dmitrieff, daughter of a Tsarist nobleman and one of the most striking revolutionaries of the century.[5] Thus, in this single illustration, he unknowingly reveals the scope of an extraordinary women's movement that played such a vital role. Each and every figure, known and unknown, stands as a symbol of the process that had given birth to this revolutionary upheaval.

On Tuesday May 23, the day before the burning of the Hotel de Ville, Houghton awoke to find the struggle taking place outside the very windows of his apartment. 'Shells were falling in the Rue Lafayette at the Square Montholon', he wrote. 'All the day the insurgents were stationed at the corners of the streets leading to the Rue Lafayette, and fired on the troops in the direction of the Opera.' On the following day he found himself caught between two opposing groups. 'Shells exploded on every side, whilst crackling noise of chassepots was unceasing'. People called to one another, telling what they could see, according to the position of their windows. Sleep was impossible. At night the sky was in flames. 'Each one asked if it would not be his turn next', wrote Houghton.

Street by street, barricade by barricade, Paris was retaken. By Sunday May 27 it was all over. Those who escaped death on the barricades were rounded up like cattle. Houghton sent off his completed woodblocks and sketches to London and left for Versailles, where huge convoys were being divided up and sent to various prison camps, to await execution or exile in penal settlements in Guiana and New Caledonia.

At this point, Houghton concluded his chronicle of the Commune and returned to London. He was back again in Versailles early in September for the reckoning which followed; to him the worst spectacle of all. Bourgeois, if bohemian, radical chic that he was, he had been horrified to witness what seemed like the opening of a modern Pandora's box. But the Versailles government appalled him. He attended the military tribunals which

The Courts-Martial at Versailles:
Petroleuses Under Trial 1871.
Wood engraving.
$8\frac{7}{8} \times 11\frac{7}{8}$.
Graphic, September 23, 1871.

tried the Council of the Commune, the Central Committee, and the so-called 'petroleuses', and saw for himself that the generals and judges worked hand-in-hand to exact a pitiless revenge. Between September 3 and 5, five women were brought before such a court and accused of setting fire to the Légion d'Honneur. This was the celebrated trial of the *petroleuses* (Elizabeth Retiffe, Josephine Marchais, Eugenie Suetens, Eulalie Papavoine and Lucie Bocquin). 'Women', writes Thomas, 'who were uneducated and quite incapable of defending themselves'. The cross-examination proved that they were not incendiaries but only ambulance nurses, yet they were given savage sentences. One has but to glance at Houghton's illustration *Petroleuses Under Trial* (September 23, 1871 : p. 293), and see the rows of villainous and cynical soldiery behind the five accused women to appreciate what he thought of them. His Versaillais officers are very much the villains of the drama; and the grim faces of the military tribunal are conceived in the same critical spirit.

Houghton would probably have agreed with Ruskin that the chief cause of the revolution lay, 'in the idleness, disobedience and covetousness of the richer and middle classes'. For Houghton, radical solutions meant liberation and individuality, not the enslavement of violence. The Commune roused in him a revulsion which came from a fear that real or actual change would get completely out of hand, and ultimately cause the breakdown of any kind of civilized order.

He had used the common people of England, or of America for that matter, as characters in his work for years, so that he was able *almost* to feel close to them, even to pity or sometimes to befriend them. The Communards, however, were totally different: angry, defiant and armed to the teeth: strong enough to hold one of the world's largest cities for two months. Houghton surveyed this motley proletarian army and concluded that they were human beings pushed beyond the reach of charitable gentleness, let alone reason. The Versaillais, on the other hand, he thought every bit as bestial, possibly even more so; thus further class conflict was inevitable.

*Sheik Hamil c.*1870.
Watercolour on board.
$29\frac{1}{2} \times 23\frac{5}{8}$. Formerly owned
by the Brothers Dalziel.
Colin Davis Collection,
Rapallo, Italy.

X: Last Years

After his experiences in America and France Houghton became more contemplative, turning away from contemporary subjects towards a more philosophic mode of expression. He entered his 36th year with a resolve to devote more time to painting and less, much less, to his work for the *Graphic*, or indeed any other periodical. He had reached the crossroads in his career. The adverse criticism of 'Graphic America' had created a mood of disenchantment with the age of printing and its faceless public.

From January 1872 until his death in November 1875, he was sustained only by the hope that he might, in creating less obvious interpretations of challenging historical incidents, find both the buyers and the recognition he longed for. Very largely Houghton's resolve was governed by a profound sense of failure. He had always thought himself a historical painter. Like other painters who had earned a living from illustration, he was irritated by the gulf which separated him not only from the successful godlike academicians of the day such as Leighton and Millais, but also from those former brothers of the woodblock of his own generation: Marks, Poynter, Walker, Burgess, Storey and others, who also worked for the Dalziels, and had now moved up in the hierarchy to become Associates or Members of the Royal Academy. Houghton had exhibited at the Academy irregularly throughout the sixties, and his work had not been unnoticed by the more discriminating critics, but the Academy and the picture-buying public were one, and no painter, however regularly he exhibited, became even an Associate unless he subjected himself to the demands of current public taste.

There are signs that although Houghton tried to do so, he eventually refused to compromise himself, indeed it is a matter of conjecture that he ever really knew how to. Regardless of how often and how hard he tried, his paintings generally received the same sort of superficial comment that had greeted the early works of the Pre-Raphaelites; the charge of 'eccentricity' had stuck.[1]

1870 saw Houghton getting back into his stride, and beginning a group of larger and much more ambitious works. The first of these was the oil, *The Vision of Sheik Hamil* (lost). It was based on his *Argosy* illustration (1866: frontispiece) for Isa Craig's ballad, and was described by the Dalziels as a 'truly grand picture'. Writing to William Bell Scott in May 1870, Dante Gabriel Rossetti thought it had 'more real affinity to high design than anything in the place'. Orientalism was in vogue, and Houghton had scored a hit. It was purchased by Strahan, and the Dalziels commissioned a watercolour replica (Colin Davis Collection).

Sheik Hamil was – if the replica is anything to go by – an extremely revealing self-portrait, which offers us a rare glimpse of what Houghton himself looked like at the age of thirty-five. The artist, who also used himself as a model for the original illustration, developed the resemblance with haunting candour. Gazing into a setting sun, he is, in every detail, the worldly sophisticate who has long since decided to live not wisely but too well. Houghton may have intended the picture to symbolize his disenchantment and continued sense of loss since Susan's death; certainly one feels his identification with the subject very strongly. But somehow Houghton's convivial self-image belied the sentiment. Francis Palgrave, the *Saturday Review*'s (June 4, 1870: p. 738) implacably hostile critic, seized on this and wrote: 'Sheik Hamil is a brute of a fellow who, though swearing eternal fidelity to a lost wife, is at heart a Bluebeard'.

In 1871 Houghton sent nothing at all to the Academy. Nevertheless, it was a good year. He became a peripheral figure in the Art Movement of the seventies; the Minton Art Pottery Studio commissioned him to design a plate,

and the Society of Painters in Water Colours elected him an associate.[2]

Increasing prosperity provided an encouraging climate for Houghton to continue painting rather than go back to illustrating. Large paintings were now the order of the day among the newly rich picture-buying public, a trend immediately noticeable after the Academy moved from Trafalgar Square to more spacious quarters at Burlington House in 1869. As mid-Victorian taste turned in this direction, many painters who had been illustrators in their younger days saw their opportunity. Lord Leighton himself, Marks, Poynter, Yeames, Walker and many others set to work to enlarge the numerous historical subjects they had caught on the woodblock: legends, stories and verse of the beauty that was Greece and the glory that was Rome, of the Middle Ages and Christian martyrdom, the Orient and the New Testament, all previously commissioned by the various weekly or monthly magazines.

Houghton was carried along by this current fashion but – like Hunt – he also wanted to make moral comment on life as he saw it; what better vehicle for this than the book familiar to so many since childhood – the Bible?

Houghton belonged to a circle of radical Bohemians whose ideas, in the words of Thompson, were more a matter of gesture and style than of practice.[3] Hostility to the aristocracy, to businessmen and philistines, to bourgeois values, to humbug and snobbery, countered by a general appeal to goodness of the heart: these principles may be presumed of the men in Houghton's circle. But Houghton's radicalism was more robust than most of these contemporaries, although unlike William Morris, he felt no inner compulsions to be an activist. He sometimes used his art to question the values of capitalist society, but was equally opposed to deeds unjustly perpetrated by those acting in the name of revolution.

A much more complicated example of these feelings now appeared in a large painting which he began to work on during the autumn and winter of 1871-2, based on the design he had made some years previously for Bickersteth's poem, 'John Baptist' published in the *Sunday Magazine*. The finished work, entitled *John the Baptist Rebuking Herod* was shown at the Academy of 1872, in the midst of social disquiet: Republican demonstrations in Trafalgar Square, and strikes by bakers, gas-stokers, building-trade workers and police. Houghton looked back to the grasping and immoral materialism of a bygone age, and linked it with the contemporary condition. Herod was a man of craft rather than strength, whose fear of political turmoil led him to execute the idealistic missionary as a troublesome rebel. As in *The Vision of Sheik Hamil*, Houghton plays the title role; it is he who opposes the tyrant and points out the wrong he has done.

John the Baptist Rebuking Herod attracted more attention than any other of Houghton's paintings.[4] Jealous recalled that it displayed insight and excellent dramatic skill:

The figure of the Baptist perhaps recalled the apostle touched with mildness and sweet persuasion, rather than a prophet filled with fire and moral severity, but the picture was vital and impressive, the spectator feeling that the Baptist's words were creeping like a frost over his auditors, the beautiful slave being rapt, Herod roused from his lethargy and lust, and the wicked woman, shapely limbed and redolent in ebon tresses, hiding her nascent vengeance under an expression of dainty and supercilious repose.

The terrible Palgrave of the *Saturday Review* (May 11, 1872: p. 601) however, not only disagreed, but chose the occasion to launch another attack on Houghton, the second that year.[5]

To be abused by the more academic critics was a burden he shared with most of his contemporaries, but unlike Pinwell, Sandys, Whistler or Doré, he was also rejected as an illustrator. He was also subjected to the inexplicable personal hostility of an influential critic, the monastic Stephens who later dismissed him as 'a heavy-handed follower of Millais whose work even at its best was sluggish, trivial and seldom spontaneous'.[6] Such hostility must have been painful to Houghton, not only because he had failed to realize an anticipated personal triumph which should have gained him election to the Academy, along with the rest of his contemporaries, but also because it denied outright his claim to be considered a serious artist. Without a doubt this double-edged rejection contributed considerably to his drinking problem.

He was fortunate in having a staunch circle of friends to comfort him in his last disillusioning years. Those closest to him were Tourrier and Pinwell, and his father, (who did not die until 1874), and his brother, William. Houghton shared his Queen's Terrace studio with Tourrier, which was only a few minutes walk from his house in King Henry's Road, Hampstead; and during 1871 the faithful Tourrier was a lodger in the house.

He continued to derive great strength from home and family, and made much of his son and daughters. Sometimes he would rush them off to the seaside, where he would make them order dinner and become masters of the revels that invariably took place. His father, failing rapidly in health after a stroke, was now confined to his chair, but always enjoyed hearing the latest gossip from the Savage Club. The old Commander's death as the result of a final stroke on May 19, 1874, was a grievous blow even though long expected; and it left 'Granny', or

*The Taproom of the Eyre Arms c.*1871-2. Wood engraving. $8\frac{7}{8} \times 11\frac{7}{8}$. Published as *Before the Bar* in the Sketches in London series, *Graphic*, May 11, 1872.

Midnight Sketches from Life 1872. Engraved by C. Roberts. $11 \times 8\frac{7}{8}$. From the front cover, *Graphic*, July 13, 1872. University Library, Cambridge. Houghton was arrested for incitement while drawing the festivities celebrating the recovery of the Prince of Wales from typhoid fever in February, 1872. He spent the night in the cells, and as a result, the *Graphic*, with certain alterations, published this series based on his experiences in Bow Street jail. (facing page)

[126]

Sophia, Houghton's disapproving mother, and his widowed sister Harriet in charge. He now began to spend more and more time away from the family in the company of Tourrier who, unlike Pinwell, did not deplore his drinking. And after the day's work they would forget their frustrations and the strictures of the critics, and carouse in the smoky taprooms of the celebrated local taverns.[7]

Houghton's dread of solitude was doubtless the cause of his gregariousness, and now he was approaching middle age it was more intense than ever. In addition to nights at the Savage Club, drinking bouts also took place at the studio, where companions and colleagues alike would fall asleep on the crowded floor. From time to time, whenever the party ran dry, a hunting horn was blown, at which the potman of the 'Eyre Arms' would drop everything and hurry over with fresh supplies. Houghton's gregariousness – if one can so describe it – extended to the poor and unfortunate.

The studio was also the venue of Dickensian entertainments, where all the tramps Houghton could possibly find were given feasts, and as much to drink as they could hold. One such event took place before Christmas, 1872, when he invited a party of unfortunates from the Islington Workhouse, and reported the festivities for the Christmas number of the *Graphic*. From the text note accompanying his illustration, *Our Artist's Christmas Entertainment* (December 28, 1872: p. 605), it appears to have been a great success. A testimonial was published from those invited, signed by 'your most Humble Servants the Cripple Leading the Blind, Thomas Wager, James Large, William Eiking and John Bayliss'. The toasts, quoted by Houghton, indicate its most convivial character: 'Here's short shoes and long corns to the enemy of the working man! The inside of a loaf, and the outside of a gaol' and finally, 'wish we could make this day last till tomorrow night!'

Such episodes must have made it much more difficult for Houghton to devote himself seriously to his work; sharing his studio with Tourrier, himself a heavy drinker (he died of apoplexy in 1892), couldn't have helped matters. Accordingly, there was a sharp increase in his drinking, although he compensated for this by slipping into the role of a 'character'. His last *Graphic* illustration,

THE GRAPHIC

AN ILLUSTRATED WEEKLY NEWSPAPER

VOL. VI.—No. 137
Regd. at General Post Office as a Newspaper]

SATURDAY, JULY 13, 1872

[PRICE SIXPENCE
Or by post Sixpence Halfpenny

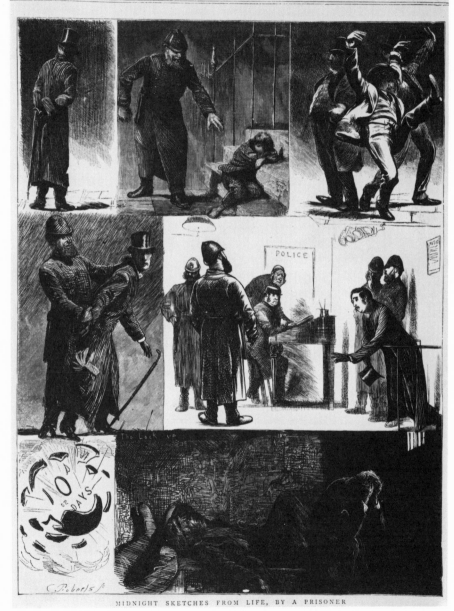

MIDNIGHT SKETCHES FROM LIFE, BY A PRISONER

Taking the Waters at Baden-Baden (October 5, 1872: p. 307), may have been the result of a visit to Germany to take a cure. But nothing further appeared, indicating that Thomas had finally given him up as a reliable contributor. Remarkably enough, there is little sign that his alcoholism had a comparable effect on his painting; although the very effort to continue working must have added considerably to the strain on his now rapidly deteriorating health. During 1873-5, he had a last burst of creative energy which produced several ambitious works.

The catalogue of the sale of the contents of his studio (Christie's, March 17, 1876) reveals that he executed a series of four paintings in oil and watercolour based on his illustrations for the *Arabian Nights* of the previous decade. In these he found, no doubt, a link with the East of his family; a refuge of wish-fulfilment, where amiable tyrants ruled and beautiful princesses with the features of Susan were offered as prizes to the brave. All but one of these are lost. The one remaining is the exquisite *Transformation of King Beder* now in the Victoria and Albert Museum.

During the summer of 1874, his condition deteriorated still further. Pinwell, who had long been concerned about his friend, was himself suffering from a pulmonary disease, and died on September 8, 1875. Houghton was present at the burial in Highgate cemetery, and as all stood around the grave he sighed, 'Ah my boys, you will be planting me here also before three months'. And he proved to be right. He died of cirrhosis on Thursday November 25, 1875, holding his little portrait of Susan in his hands.[8] It was the end of one of the least recognized artists of the Victorian era: unrecognized in more ways than one. By the end of 1972, the black marble cross which had marked his grave had tumbled down in disrepair, and the elaborate lead letters of his name had long been vandalised. After due notice was given, the gravestone was removed and the site cleared and levelled off. A small metal plaque took its place: number 4846. It was as if time itself had taken part in the conspiracy to expunge all trace of Arthur Boyd Houghton.

Houghton was an artist unlike his contemporaries. Many knew him, if at all, simply as one of a group containing such illustrious names as du Maurier, Pinwell, Sandys and Walker, associating him with magazines like *Good Words* and books such as the Dalziels' *Arabian Nights*. As a painter he made a modest but important contribution to nineteenth century realism. As a draughtsman alone he ventured out of mid-Victorian England to penetrate the new changing world. So thousands more who were unaware of his name would know more about Mormons, Shakers and buffalo-hunting, or what the Commune was really like, from his illustrations in the *Graphic* – Houghton's charged personal vision of such events.

Such a vision was all the more remarkable because illustration in his lifetime was largely a black and white art. Later in his career however, he indulged his craving for colour especially in the paintings of oriental subjects; using a rich colour range suited to the mood of each subject, mostly warm yellows and browns with vermillion or Prussian blue accents. *Lalla Rookh* (Gallichen collection) is a good example of this later palette. Houghton's handling of pigment itself – largely derived from the Pre-Raphaelites – vacillated between the highly finished realism of *Holborn in 1861* to the flowing looser brushwork of *Sheik Hamil* and *The Transformation of King Beder*.

The heavy responsibility which rested on his one and only eye caused him early on in his career to leave out what was superfluous in a design. He used the one eye almost like a wide-angle lens to encompass what he saw. He made the discovery that Japanese prints could help him simplify the composing of forms on a two-dimensional surface. The notion that a picture could be made up of dominant, sometimes silhouetted shapes on a white or low-keyed background not only made it physically easier for him to make a design, but increase the power of its image. An outstanding example of Houghton's success with this kind of composition is *Coasting at Omaha*. All the black foreground figures are placed elliptically against a white hillside; but their weight would pull the picture down were it not for the whirling lines of blown snow in the background. The total result is not the static equilibrium which characterized so much of Victorian illustration, but a composition of intensely dramatic movement.

Artists revere those among them who are strong

enough to withstand compromise. Houghton became a symbol, 'an artist's artist', even for the many too young to have known his name when he was alive. He was remembered as an iconoclast who persisted in making moral judgements on society in a personal and idiosyncratic manner. Of those who came later in the nineties, there were few to whom Houghton was not a source of inspiration; Houseman, Rackham and Sullivan in England, and Abbey, Pyle and N. C. Wyeth in the United States; all of whom contributed to the magazines and books of yet another graphic renaissance.

[129]

Perhaps the most perceptive comment was made by Vincent van Gogh, in a letter (262) to Theo:

He was of that club of draughtsmen [of which] it was said at the time, 'it is too good to last'. I often disliked many things in England, but that black-and-white and Dickens are things that make up for it all ... His woodcuts might also pass for etchings. The world says, 'too good to last', but for that reason because it is rare the *good* lasts. It is not produced every day, it will never be got mechanically, but what is, is, and that is not lost but lasts.

The Transformation of King Beder 1874. Watercolour on board. $19\frac{1}{2} \times 23\frac{1}{2}$. The subject, a story from the *Arabian Nights*, 'The History of Prince Beder and Princess Giauhare', is based on a similar design by the artist, published in *Dalziels' Arabian Nights*, 1865, and entitled, 'King Beder transformed into a Bird'. Victoria & Albert Museum, London.

Notes

CHAPTER I

1. According to the Indian Navy Fund Family Register, India Office Records (L/A6/23/18/2/15), Houghton was born March 13, 1836 in the Nilgiris. The *East India Register*, 1837, 111, states the place of birth as Kotagherry (*sic*). A certificate of birth in the possession of the artist's grandson, Mr Davis, reveals that he was privately baptized into the Church of England at Kotagiri, Nilgiris.

2. The Houghtons moved house every few years until each son was launched on a professional career of some kind. In 1837 they lived at Parson's Green, an enclave of the gentry in the suburban district of Fulham, near London. By 1838 they had moved on further west to Kingston-on-Thames. In 1842 they were resident at St Helier, Jersey. But by 1844 they were back in the London area, and from September 1852 to May 1863 (their longest stay anywhere) they lived as the first occupants of a large and handsome detached house at 7 Clifton Road East (now Clifton Hill), St John's Wood, then, as now, a fashionable suburb.

3. William Robert Houghton (1826-97) entered the Bombay Native Infantry as a cadet in 1842, rising to the rank of Lieut.-General in 1888. He travelled widely through the Bombay Presidency, recording his impressions in watercolours of great delicacy and poetic intensity. William maintained contact with the family throughout his army career, spending his furloughs with them whenever possible.

4. James Mathew Leigh (1808-60) was the son of Samuel Leigh, a well-known publisher. He was the only pupil accepted by William Etty, the celebrated English exponent of the neo-classical nude. Later he completed his apprenticeship in France, Italy and Germany. Impressed by the 'master-classes' of Düsseldorf and especially those of Paris, he asked Etty's advice and received his encouragement to establish an atelier of the Parisian style in London. Dissatisfied with English art education, he sought to 'correct the tendency of the English Style towards weakness of design, effeminacy of composition and flauntiness of colouring'. Like his master, Leigh's art derived from Titian and Rubens to produce allegorical pictures of doubtful quality. He had shown these for many years at the Royal Academy with little success. He found solace in propagating his ideas about drawing and contributing unsigned reviews of current exhibitions.

5. At Leigh's, Houghton made many friends and acquaintances with whom he remained in touch throughout his life. Those closest to him were: Alfred Holst Tourrier (1836-92), historical painter and illustrator of Hugenot origin; Thomas Morten (1836-66), painter and illustrator, a contributor to the magazines of the sixties and illustrator of several books; George Walter Thornbury (1828-76), who abandoned art for a literary career and wrote the worst biography of Turner in the English language. He was also acquainted with Henry Stacy Marks (leading light of the St John's Wood Clique), John Bagnold Burgess and George Adolphus Storey.

6. Previously known as the Clipstone Street Society, the Langham had been famous as a Sketching Club for more established artists for almost twenty-five years (members included the genre painters Topham and Goodall, as well as the illustrators Tenniel and Keene). The first years of the Clipstone Street Club, like the Sketching Society founded by Girtin, Cotman and their circle, had coincided with an earlier revolt against the sterile teaching methods of the Academy.

7. The enormous number of pictures shown at the big London exhibitions in the Victorian era was enough to daunt the most optimistic young artist. At the Portland Gallery in 1859 some 600 works were shown; the Society of British Artists annual averaged 1,000; both were dwarfed by the Royal Academy's 3,500.

CHAPTER II

1. The life of Arthur Herbert, Houghton's son, also ended in tragic circumstances. After completing his education, he emigrated to Australia sometime during the 1880s, but met with a riding accident which damaged his spine. He returned to England where he lived with his sister, Georgina Maud, and her family for about a year before he died in the 1900s. (Mr Davis, in a letter to the author, September 7, 1972.)

2. 162 King Henry's Road was demolished in 1968, to make way for the Swiss Cottage Holiday Inn.

3. According to Mr Davis, Houghton was 'a life-long member'.

4. See Harry Furniss, *My Bohemian Days*, Chapter VI, p. 75. The celebrated *Punch* caricaturist pens an amusing description of the stormy debates which took place at the Coger's Hall in the 1870s.

5. Lionel Charles Henley (1843-93). Painter and illustrator, who had been a 'boisterous and entertaining' fellow-student of du Maurier's at Düsseldorf, *c*.1859-60, where he formed, with du Maurier and Tom Armstrong, a lively trio. He shared rooms with du Maurier (85 Newman Street) until June 1861,

but later shocked some of his friends by marrying his ex-mistress who was regarded as a 'fallen woman' (see Ormond, *du Maurier*, pp. 98, 111, 204). Henley was a frequent contributor to *Fun*, and occasionally to other illustrated magazines.

6. Life, '*That Unfortunate Young Man Morten*', pp. 369-402. Unless otherwise stated, my account of the Morten fund is drawn from this authoritative account largely based on the Angeli-Penkill Papers, University of British Columbia, Vancouver.

7. Pinwell's life was, from beginning to end, straight out of Dickens. Born in 1842, he was six years younger than Houghton. His father, a building contractor, died when he was a child. His mother, an illiterate countrywoman, sent him out to work as a butterman's boy when he should have been at school. A high-spirited personality, he saved enough to attend evening drawing classes at the St Martin's Lane School, where he was fortunate in meeting Fred Walker; from there he went with Walker to Leigh's (at this time Heatherly's). Then he worked for the cheaper magazines before being recruited by the Dalziels to make woodblock designs to *Good Words*, the *Sunday Magazine* and the *Graphic*.

CHAPTER III

1. Some indication of the level of that income can be gained from the fact that the twenty more prolific illustrators of the sixties contributed at least fifteen illustrations a year to each of the three leading magazines, *Once A Week*, *Cornhill* and *Good Words*, between 1860-70. (Hence the reason why illustration acted as a magnet to so many struggling young artists.) In 1862, *London Society* began publication; by 1865 three more highly successful magazines, *Argosy*, *Sunday Magazine* and *The Quiver* were on sale, not to mention the boom in illustrated books. The minimal rate for a full-page drawing averaged £9.00; and a half-page, £4.50. This would give these twenty artists a basic annual income of £405.00, which would have certainly risen to at least £1,000 by 1865. The mid-Victorian pound was worth about £30.00 in 1980, and during that period a family could live well in a large house on £500-600 a year and afford both a cook and a parlourmaid.

2. Other famous illustrators who were contemporaries of Houghton include: Edward Lear (1812-88), traveller, author and illustrator of *The Book of Nonsense* (1846); John Tenniel (1820-1914), painter and caricaturist, illustrator of the Alice books of Lewis Carroll, *Alice in Wonderland* (1865) and *Through the Looking Glass* (1871); Richard Doyle (1824-83), who chiefly illustrated fairy tales and published books of annotated drawings, including *The Foreign Tour of Brown, Jones and Robinson* (1854); and Walter Crane (1845-1915), whose toy-book, *Sing a Song of Sixpence* (1866), introduced the first use of flat colour to the illustration of books.

3. 'A Great Publisher from the North of Scotland', *Inverness Courier*, December 29, 1903: p. 3.

4. His first published illustration appeared in the short-lived monthly, *Entertaining Things*. The subject was a 'Real-Life' story of unrequited love, 'The

Maid of the Woolpack', by Andrew Haliday (January, 1862: p. 9). In a luxuriantly autumnal setting a beautiful but distraught girl lies against a tree on which her lover's initials are carved. Millais' influence predominates and even the top of the woodblock is arched in the best Pre-Raphaelite style. Although small in size, it is an image of disturbing intensity, engraved with great fidelity by the Dalziels. His first book was no less conspicuously successful aesthetically; a set of four full-page illustrations act as a perfect complement to the unquiet quality of Wilkie Collins' macabre tales, *After Dark* (1862).

5. Dr Thomas Guthrie (1803-73), the first editor of the *Sunday Magazine* (1864-73), was a celebrated Scots divine. A Liberal, he was active in the social movements of the Mid-Victorian period, and helped found the ragged schools.

6. Before joining the *Graphic*'s team, Houghton, during the autumn of 1866, accepted an offer to join the freelance staff of *Fun*, the Liberal counterpart of *Punch*. Against his better judgement, from November 1866 to August 1867 he contributed a weekly full-page political cartoon, in the magisterial manner of Tenniel's big *Punch* page. But 'Notwithstanding [his] great ability,' wrote the Dalziels, 'his quality of mind hardly fitted him to join in with Tom Hood's idea of the punctuality indispensable for conducting a weekly periodical.' Hood himself was partly to blame for not realizing that Houghton's true bent was social, not political, satire, which the artist *himself* had to initiate. *Fun*, unlike the successful *Punch*, never resolved such problems. Founded in 1863, it thrived on reform, but lacked distinctive graphic appeal.

CHAPTER IV

1. Since he was a young man, Thomas had dreamed of establishing his own picture paper; he had spent the years 1846-8 in New York and Boston assisting his older brother, the artist George Henry Thomas, on two short-lived ventures, *The Republic* and *The Historical Picture Gallery*. As head of the engraving department of the *Illustrated London News*, he gained the experience which enabled him to carry out a scheme for a rival journal supported by a group of highly-placed but disillusioned Liberals on the older paper. According to Hatton, however, the *Graphic* was projected as a rival because of a sense of personal annoyance and injury in relations between the Thomases and the Ingrams. G. H. Thomas had been a famous Special Artist on *ILN*. After his death William projected a book of drawings for the benefit of his widow and family. He asked for a loan of the blocks and was refused; a factor which led to him making his final decision to launch the *Graphic*. (Hatton, *Journalistic London*, pp. 238-9.)

2. Thomas, in a letter to Fildes, dated September 6, 1869; kindly supplied by Bernard Myers, Royal College of Art.

3. Thomas cites the figure of £20 as payment to Fildes for his drawing, *Houseless and Hungry*, in a letter to the artist dated September 6, 1869. Holl, however, was paid thirty guineas (£31.50) for his *Third Class*. (Reynolds, *Life and Work of Frank Holl*, London, 1912, p. 97.)

4. When *Houseless and Hungry* became *The Casuals*, the picture of the year at the Royal Academy of 1874, Fildes found himself launched on a long and

highly successful career capped with a knighthood. The career of Hubert von Herkomer (1849-1914), an immigrant from Bavaria, was no less impressive. He, too, became a most successful painter from re-working his *Graphic* pages as huge oils, an esteemed portrait painter and Royal Academician; and he, too, received a knighthood. Frank Holl (1845-88) also became a well known portrait painter and Royal Academician. Holl made so much money from portraiture in the last decade of his short life that he had Norman Shaw design and build two houses, one in London and the other in Surrey. Fildes, at the *Graphic*'s coming-of-age dinner in 1890, spoke of Thomas' great role in sustaining that most English Art, that of the Illustrator, 'who by earnest and sincere efforts arrests, stirs, or gives pleasure to the many'. Herkomer was more personal in his tribute. Writing in *The Times* on the occasion of Thomas' death in 1900, he looked back on his early career, admitting that he owed everything to him; that the whole experience of the *Graphic* 'was a lesson in life, a lesson in art'. Holl's son wrote that the *Graphic* gave his father much-needed self-confidence and concentration: 'The mere fact of having to have the block ready to the moment when the *Graphic* messenger presented himself at the studio door, gave him the necessary impetus.'

CHAPTER V

1. Thomas' first choice was the young and relatively unknown Fildes, whose *Houseless and Hungry* had attracted so much attention. 'I believe you would make your fortune,' Thomas wrote to Fildes (September 27, 1869). 'I could give you first rate letters of introduction out there.' Fildes, however, resisted the temptation and, dazzled by the prospect of working for the great Dickens, refused the assignment.

2. The Fifth Avenue Hotel stood on Fifth Avenue between 23rd and 24th Streets facing Madison Square. Flanked on the east and north by the great mansions of the wealthy, it had been the home of politicians and businessmen ever since the Prince of Wales had given it a send-off by staying there in 1860. During Houghton's stay, the hotel would have been at its busiest. During autumn, as in the spring, merchants from all parts of New England, the South and the Midwest flocked to New York to order goods from the great downtown emporia on Broadway. The hotel was demolished in 1908.

3. Houghton referred to his 'American friends' but mentioned none by name. William Waud (c.1830-78), an English illustrator who had joined his older artist brother, Alfred Waud, in America during the fifties, may have befriended Houghton. William was living at 52 John Street, New York City. His name and address were scribbled in the artist's pocket sketchbook. Waud was familiar with America from his travels as a well-known Special for *Harper's Weekly* during and after the Civil War. He was at this time depicting the New York social scene himself. It is likely that he advised his fellow-countryman and accompanied him on some of his walks about the city. Waud may also have introduced Houghton to the New York circle of Englishmen, or Americans born in England. These included Charles Parsons, the much beloved chief of *Harper's* art department, and Frank Bellew, caricaturist and illustrator, a former contributor to *Punch* who had emigrated in 1850. Thomas Nast, the

leading staff cartoonist of *Harper's Weekly*, would have also been a likely acquaintance. Nast lived in Harlem near Fifth Avenue, and was a devotee of that dashing American pastime, harness racing or trotting. Races were held at the nearby Grand Circuit Harlem lane track. Nast may have invited Houghton to accompany him to view what had become a big business sport after the Civil War. This resulted in the half-page illustration, *Trotting, Eighth Avenue, New York* (April 23, 1870: p. 489).

4. Houghton's letters to his parents and his children – enlivened with comic sketches – must have told a great deal more of his feelings about America. What happened to them is a complete mystery. His youngest daughter Cecily thought they had been treasured by her grandmother but after her death they could not be found and were assumed to have been destroyed, as was so much of what belonged to the artist.

5. Charles Parsons (1821-1910). Born Hampshire, England. Emigrated to America with his family, 1830. Assumed management of *Harper's* art department 1863, and established the Franklin Square group: a brilliant band of young illustrators which included Edwin Austin Abbey, Howard Pyle, William Allen Rogers and Winslow Homer, all of whom took the English illustrators of the sixties as their models. Lucas quotes Abbey as seeing Houghton in the art department of *Harper's* prior to his return to England. Houghton had brought his Western woodblocks to show Parsons. Presumably they had met before Houghton left New York on his western travels. (*Charles Parsons and His Domain*, introduction; Lucas, *Edwin Austin Abbey*, I, pp. 14-15.)

6. Campaign or 'torchlight' parades were a familiar sight at election times. They were usually held at night to achieve maximum dramatic effect. Local political organizations – Democrat and Republican – designed their own uniforms and regalia. The Marching Clubs competed with one another in creating unusual costumes and floats, but the Democrats, with a far greater variety of ethnic groups, usually won. Houghton shows one such group in the ceremonial uniform of an English Guards regiment, complete with fur hats, or 'bearskins'.

7. Houghton had depicted an old German ragwoman pulling a cart piled with junk, watched by a yawning Irish policeman. Published as *In the Rag Trade* (April 9, 1870, p. 437), this may have been the illustration that prompted a visiting New Yorker to make a personal protest. Thomas quotes the incident in his article, 'The Making of the *Graphic*', as taking place at a Liverpool railway bookstall. After buying his *Graphic*, the American tourist shook his fist at the astonished attendant, shouting, 'It's a lie, sir, an infernal lie!' *Harper's Weekly* (May 7, 1870), however, put things right by publishing the same engraving, substituting a young, handsome, and alert guardian of the law for Houghton's lounging cop!

8. The *Weekly* may have had in mind the half-page illustration *New York Police* (March 26, 1870: p. 393), an irreverent characterization of the husky Broadway Squad, one of the city's sights. Houghton could not have touched on a more sensitive spot. 'Nebulae' of *Galaxy* (Apr l, 1870) was particularly

incensed. 'It is rare', he raged, 'that an artist of any pretensions imitates humanity so abominably. The Broadway Squad is a fine body of picked men, well knit, athletic, and of admirable carriage. Mr Houghton's sketch makes them a set of lanky, ill-made travesties on the human form. . . .'

9. The name itself arose from its associations; it was a massive Egyptian Revival edifice designed by the English architect, John Haviland, and built in 1838 on the site of a pre-Revolutionary gallows. Dickens, who had visited the place in 1842, described it as 'a dismal-fronted pile of bastard Egyptian, like an enchanter's palace in melodrama'. It was demolished in 1897.

CHAPTER VI

1. At the time of Houghton's visit, New Lebanon was the largest of some eighteen Shaker communes, with a membership of between 500-600, organized in eight families. (Andrews, *The People Called Shakers*, pp. 290-1.)

2. Houghton appears to have made friends with Fraser, as he made a note in his sketchbook to send him a copy of John Stuart Mill's *On Liberty*. (*Sketchbook*: 7.)

3. Houghton arrived in Boston on November 15. There is a reference to James R. Osgood (probably his host) and the pencilled note, '*Atlantic Monthly*' in his sketchbook. At that time Osgood was the publisher of the *Atlantic*, and the active partner in the well-known publishing firm of McIlvaine, Fields and Osgood. He was a great lover of England and all things English, and travelled back and forth across the Atlantic regularly on co-publishing ventures; he was, in addition, a generous patron of artists. Osgood was also the publisher of *Every Saturday* (edited by Thomas Bailey Aldrich), which he had recently transformed into a picture paper; he had, that very month, increased its size to reprint the electrotypes supplied by the *Graphic*; and in its pages 'Graphic America' would very shortly take pride of place.

4. Frederick Edwin Church (1826-1900) was a celebrated member of the Hudson River School of landscape painters, who distilled on huge canvases the romantic essences of the wonders of nature. His *Niagara* (Corcoran Gallery of Art, Washington, D.C.), painted in 1857, was considered his masterpiece.

CHAPTER VII

1. George Catlin (1795-1872), the American painter of the Indian and the Old West, exerted a constant influence on Victorian painters and illustrators interested in the West. His two-volume classic, profusely illustrated, *Letters and Notes on the Manners, Customs and Conditions of the North American Indian* (London, 1841, 1866), was a perennial Victorian bestseller.

2. At the invitation of William Slafter of Tuscola, Michigan, Houghton made a side excursion from Chicago. Slafter, a New Englander from Vermont, had established a farm along the Cass River and was in Chicago to buy various tools and supplies. He invited the artist to spend Christmas with his family and try his hand at shooting turkeys. The trip took Houghton on the Michigan Southern east to Pontiac; then north by the Flint and Père Marquette Railroad to Birch Run, a station some eight miles from Tuscola, a small village. The artist stayed at McPherson's Hotel and after the Christmas festivities, went forth with Slafter, his son Alonzo, and the innkeeper, John McPherson, to look for turkeys in a vast primeval forest. The spectacle enthralled him, surrounded as they were by enormous pine trees, blotting out the daylight. Huge charred stumps, the aftermath of autumn fires, added to the enchantment; a scene he afterwards redrew as the dramatic full-page, *Shooting Turkeys in an American Forest* (December 23, 1871: p. 605). The turkeys proved to be elusive. 'We unfortunately sallied forth without dogs,' wrote Houghton, 'which was simply fun for the bubbley jocks as without the canine element they lie as close and as still as hares.'

CHAPTER VIII

1. While Houghton was still in the East, the first instalment of Buntline's serial appeared in the *Boston Transcript* (December 15, 1869) and in the *New York Weekly* (December 23, 1869). Widely advertised, this was probably read by the artist, thus arousing his interest in Cody, as well as the hope of meeting him on his trip through the West.

2. See W. F. Cody (Buffalo Bill), *The Life of William F. Cody* (Hartford 1879), p. 286. 'During the winter of 1869-70, I spent a great deal of time in pursuit of game, and during the season, we had two hunting parties of Englishmen there, one party being that of Mr [Lord] Flynn, and the other of George [*sic*] Boyd Houghton of London.'

3. Record of Events, February 1870, Post Returns, Fort McPherson, National Archives, Washington, D.C.

4. The artist's companion was, from his appearance, probably Lord Flynn, whom Houghton met in Chicago. He appears in *Taking a Nap*, *Pawnees Gambling*, *A Smoke with Friendlies* and *Crossing a Canyon*. This was the 'Mr Flynn' referred to by Cody in his autobiography, but Cody's memory is known to have been unreliable. There may therefore have been only 'a (single) party of Englishmen, most prominent of whom was Boyd Houghton . . .' as stated by Leonard and Goodman.

5. Helen Cody Westmore, in her reminiscences, *The Last of the Great Scouts*, relates that she accompanied her brother on a buffalo hunt in the spring of 1870. As women were rarely, if ever, invited to join such expeditions, she is probably the mounted female in the right background of the illustration *Camping Out*.

6. See *Sketchbook*: 2, 'What Cheer Home, San Fran.'

7. *Harper's Weekly* was now sharing the American rights of the series with *Every Saturday*, and to save time while waiting for his passage home, he had several engraved by Measom, and left stereotypes with Parsons. The celebrated American illustrator, Edwin Austin Abbey, then a sixteen-year-old apprentice in the art department, recalled Houghton bringing 'all his boxwood with him'. Houghton's blocks aroused widespread interest as they were

screwed together with brass screws, steel or iron being used in America.

CHAPTER IX

1. At 1 Queen's Terrace, NW6, just off the Finchley Road. It is now a garage.

2. The latest recruit to the *Graphic*'s freelance staff, young Sydney Prior Hall, was already on his way to the front. Another Special, John Leighton ('Luke Limner'), would cover day-to-day stories in Paris, sending sketches and information for finished illustrations to be drawn on the woodblock by staff illustrators, or 'Home Artists'. See Hall, *Sketches from an Artist's Portfolio*, and Leighton, *Paris Under the Commune*.

3. *Graphic*, June 17, 1871: p. 571: a text note quoting Houghton which accompanied two sketches redrawn by Macbeth and Small.

4. Nathalie Lemel, a 25-year-old ex-bookbinder, was a leading member of the Central Committee of the militant *Union des Femmes*, the women's section of the French International. She was sentenced to penal servitude in Polynesia. Thomas adds that 'Nathalie Lemel had gone, on the orders of the Commune, with about fifty women to defend the barricades of Les Batignolles and the Place Pigalle (Montmartre).'

5. Elizabeth Dmitrieff, whose elegant profile can be seen at the extreme right of Houghton's illustration, was the daughter of a former Hussar officer and landowner, Louka Kouchelev. As a student in St Petersburg she became involved in the underground against Tsardom. After leaving Russia, she married a Colonel Tomanovsky in order to complete her education at the University of Geneva. She spoke several languages and visited London during the summer of 1870, where she met Marx and formed a friendship with him and his daughters. Under her leadership, the *Union des Femmes* was formed in April 1871.

CHAPTER X

1. At the Royal Academy of 1867, Houghton had shown *Boy Martyrs*, an oil version of his Goya-like illustration of an episode in the struggle for religious freedom in fifteenth-century Germany (*Sunday Magazine*, 1867: p. 256). It failed to attract any attention. He followed this up in 1868 with a portrait of Henry Bassett, a prominent member of the Chemical Society. Portraiture, as many of Houghton's colleagues had discovered, was certain to bring in a much larger income than woodblock illustration. William Rossetti, who praised the painting in his *Academy Notes* (1868: p. 8) as a 'capital piece of peculiarity', probably did him a disservice. Then in 1869 he sent in *A.D.1580* (now lost), a picture representing a dandy admiring himself in a mirror. It was satirical in flavour, but Dante Gabriel thought it 'absolutely vulgar'. The *Art Journal* (May 1869: p. 171), always friendly to him, praised it as a work 'painted with amazing power and brilliance'.

2. Houghton sent three works to the spring exhibition: *Old Friends*, *Hiawatha and Minnehaha*, and *In Captivity*. Again the critics were provoked by the aura of eccentricity surrounding his subjects. *Hiawatha and Minnehaha*, probably his worst picture, came in for strong disapproval. In addition to Stephens' caustic comment (*Athenaeum*, May 6, 1871: p. 566), 'Pictures of savages are rarely good for anything but ethnological diagrams', was Tom Taylor's remark in *The Times* (May 6, 1871). 'The picture' added Taylor, 'might serve a more useful purpose as a processional banner for some Women's Rights Association'. *In Captivity* (now lost), hung in the place of honour, was received favourably. The *Illustrated London News* (April 29, 1871: p. 422) described the picture as a procession of turbanned figures escorting two handsome women in eastern costume, guarded by swarthy sentinels in conical helmets, posted along adjacent mounds of earth, armed with scourges. It was, in the words of the *Graphic* (May 6, 1871: p. 415), 'carefully and brilliantly painted'.

3. Thompson was discussing the circle of Henry Mayhew, but his words can equally be applied to Houghton. (Edward P. Thompson & Eileen Yeo, *The Unknown Mayhew*.)

4. The art critic of the *Illustrated London News* (May 25, 1872: p. 503) went as far as to describe it as 'one of the most original and powerful conceptions in the exhibition', and compared it favourably to 'the most obviously studied and often over-crowded archaeological restorations of Alma Tadema'. The *Art Journal* (1872: p. 201) considered it a superior work, 'with the execution of a quality which ought to have caused the painting to be hung in one of the best places in the Academy'. Tom Taylor, writing in the *Graphic* (June 29, 1872: p. 606) thought it 'a zealous attempt to depart from the conventionalism in dealing with a scriptural scene'. Regrettably, the painting is now lost, and only available in the emasculated form of an indifferent wood-engraving, published in the *Graphic* in 1876, after the artist's death.

5. Francis Turner, or, as he was known, Francis Palgrave, persecuted the British artist in the *Saturday Review* from 1866, 'which made him', wrote Henry Adams in his *Education of Henry Adams* (1918), 'the most unpopular man in London'. After saying that the weakest works in the Academy were those concerned with religion, Palgrave attacked Houghton for erring in the opposite direction! (*John the Baptist Rebuking Herod*', he wrote, 'is in a style more profane than sacred. Herod and the Baptist are so disfigured as to raise a smile; the whole composition seems to pertain to the region of comedy . . . his [Houghton's] work does not lie in the Holy Land but in America; an Indian with a tomahawk is more in his way than a prophet or a King.'

6. *Athenaeum*, 1, 1897: p. 515.

7. These included the 'Eyre Arms', Finchley Road (now demolished), the headquarters of the St John's Wood Clique, and 'The Knights of St John' (which still stands), its overflow in Queen's Terrace. In the summer they would walk to Hampstead and spend the day drinking beer and port in the pleasantly shaded gardens of 'Jack Straw's Castle'.

8. As stated on Certificate DX 073072, General Register Office, London.

Appendix I

Select List of Works in Public Collections

GREAT BRITAIN

BEDFORD. Cecil Higgins Art Gallery: an early watercolour and gouache drawing, *Caught in the Act*, c.1858-60; and *Helga and Hildebrand*, a woodblock drawing for *Ballad Stories of the Affections*. Cambridge. Fitzwilliam Museum: *Job*, pen study for Dalziel Bible, c.1863. The Print Room has complete collection of 'Graphic America' from the *Graphic*, 1869-74.

CAMBRIDGE. University Library: possesses majority of the books containing illustrations by the artist, especially the Dalziel Fine Art series in their original case bindings; also a presentation copy of the Dalziel Bible pulled on India paper and a good collection of the magazines, many unbound in their original covers.

LONDON. The British Museum: pencil study of a donkey with figures, c.1861. Study for donkey in illustration, *The Favourite Visiting the Merchant of Bagdad, Dalziels' Arabian Nights* I, 197. The Print Room possesses a unique master collection of the illustrations for books and magazines, 1861-70, in 'India Proofs of Wood-Engravings by the Brothers Dalziel', XV, XVII-XX. The British Library has the most complete collection of books and magazines containing the illustrations.

LONDON. Courtauld Institute, The Witt Library: good but incomplete collection (Cornish Collection) of pages from books and magazines containing the illustrations, including 'Graphic America' and the cartoons from *Fun*.

LONDON. Kenwood House Museum: an excellent collection of choice early oils in the Iveagh Bequest, including: *Recruits* (The Recruiting Party), 1859; *The Deserter*, 1859; *Volunteers Marching Out*, 1860; *Itinerant Singers* (Poor Nomads), 1860-1; *London Street Scene*, 1860-1; also an early work and the *Scene from All's Well that Ends Well*, c.1860.

LONDON. Royal Academy of Arts: complete set of illustrations for the *Arabian Nights*.

LONDON. Tate Gallery: a most important general collection. The paintings are representative of most periods and include: *The Don on the Island*, c.1857-8; *Punch and Judy*, c.1860; *Volunteers*, c.1860; *Lady with a Book*, 1860-1; *Ramsgate Sands* (Out of Doors), 1863; *Mother and Children Reading*, 1863; and a miscellaneous collection of excellent watercolour drawings, pencil studies; a large selection of woodblock drawings for illustrations, and proofs.

LONDON. Victoria & Albert Museum: an important general collection. Some good examples of the artist's later manner: *Don Quixote and Rozinante* (The Don's Discretion), 1869; *Hiawatha and Minnehaha*, 1871; *The Transformation of King Beder*, 1873-4; and *An Oriental with Performing Monkeys* (A Mendicant), 1874.

In the Print Room, the collection is reinforced by thirteen pencil studies for the *Dalziels' Arabian Nights* illustrations; and there is an extensive selection of pages and proofs of book and magazine illustrations. The Print Room also possesses the artist's pocket sketchbook, containing sketches and addresses made and noted on his travels in eastern and western United States, October 1869-March 1870. The Art Library possesses the majority of the books and magazines containing the illustrations, many of the books being in their original case bindings.

OXFORD. The Ashmolean Museum of Art & Archaeology: an excellent oil, *Interior with Children Playing* (The Playmates), 1869.

AMERICA

MASSACHUSETTS. Cambridge, Fogg Art Museum, Harvard University: three good examples, and the largest group of the paintings in the United States: *Here i' the Sands*, 1860-1; *Interior with Mother and Child*, 1861; and *On the Beach* (The Donkey Ride), 1862.

MASSACHUSETTS. Boston, Museum of Fine Arts: the most important general collection in America; although it does not include paintings, there are watercolour drawings, pencil studies and published illustrations. Originally part of the vast Hartley Collection of the Illustrators of the Sixties, purchased in its entirety by the Museum in 1927; the two watercolours are the superb *Jewel Box*, 1868 and *The Oyster Stall*, c.1866-7; also a large collection of pencil studies for 'Graphic America', with India proofs and complete set of pages clipped from the *Graphic*; and a good selection of pencil studies, proofs and pages of illustrations for books and magazines.

NEW YORK. New York City, Metropolitan Museum of Art: a set of the 'Graphic America' illustrations.

NEW YORK. New York City, Public Library: has the *Graphic* volumes containing 'Graphic America', the Boston weekly, *Every Saturday* and the New York *Harper's Weekly* which reprinted or reproduced many of the illustrations; the library's extensive collections of Victorian books also includes many of the books and some of the magazines containing the illustrations.

WASHINGTON, D.C. The Folger Shakespeare Library: has *Toby Belch, Viola and Aguecheek*, c.1854: the artist's earliest known work, a scene from *Twelfth Night*.

AUSTRALIA

PERTH. Western Australian Art Gallery: *The Lea*, a watercolour landscape; *Street Scene*, a pen and ink drawing; and proofs of the wood-engravings, *Kiss*

Me for 'Childhood' and the illustration for 'About Toys', both from *Good Words*.

CANADA

ONTARIO. Ottawa, National Gallery of Canada: various pencil studies of the artist's children and sisters; a pencil study for an unidentified illustration; and a pencil study for a figure in *Service in the Mormon Tabernacle, Salt Lake City* (*Graphic*, 4, 1871: pp. 228–9).

ALBERTA. Calgary. The Riveredge Foundation: has incomplete collection of original pages of 'Graphic America' illustrations, supplemented by an almost complete set of photographs.

SOUTH AFRICA

JOHANNESBURG. City Art Gallery: an early example of the artist's scenes of family life: *Ramsgate Sands* (On the Sands), *c.*1860–1.

Appendix II

Select List of Publications containing Illustrations

Arranged chronologically, except where related subjects are grouped together, under the following headings: Monthly Magazines, Books, and Weekly Magazines & Newspapers. All published in London unless otherwise stated. Number of illustrations contributed follows the title of periodical or book.

MONTHLY MAGAZINES
Entertaining Things   1   1861
London Society   10   1862–8
Good Words   40   1862–8; 1871–2
Churchman's Family Magazine   1   1865
The Quiver   13   1865–8
The Argosy   2   1866–7
Sunday Magazine   57   1865–71
Routledge's Magazine for Boys   6   1866
Tinsley's Magazine   3   1867–8
The Broadway   1   1868
Golden Hours   1   1868
Good Words for the Young   7   1868–71

BOOKS
VERSE
L. Fletcher, *Christian Lyrics*   25   (Sampson Low, 1864). Reprinted in Warne's Chandos Classics, 1868
H. W. Dulcken (ed), *Home Thoughts & Home Scenes*   35   (Routledge, 1865, 1868). Reprinted as *Happy Day Stories*, 1875
A Round of Days   19   (Routledge, 1866)
R. Buchanan, *Ballad Stories of the Affections*   3   (Routledge, 1866)
Golden Thoughts from Golden Fountains   12   (Warne, 1867)
The Broadway Annual   1   (Routledge, 1867)

The Spirit of Praise   3   (Warne, 1867)
Jean Ingelow, *Poems*   16   (Longmans, Green & Dyer)
Touches of Nature by Eminent Artists & Authors   5   (Strahan, 1867)
Idyllic Pictures   3   (London & New York: Cassell, 1867). A reprinted anthology of verse and illustrations from *The Quiver*
R. Buchanan, *North Coast and Other Poems*   13   (London & New York: Routledge, 1868)
Byron, *Poetical Works*   4   (Popular Poets: Warne, 1868)
L. Valentine (ed.), *The Nobility of Life: Its Graces and Virtues*   6   (London & New York: Warne, 1869)
Picture Poesies   11   (Routledge, 1874). The majority of both verse and illustrations appeared in *A Round of Days* and *Wayside Poesies*, out of print at time of publication
Arthur William Edgar O'Shaughnessy, *Toyland*   1   (Daldy, 1875)
G. W. Thornbury (comp.), *Historical & Legendary Ballads and Songs*   1   (Chatto & Windus, 1876)
Longfellow, *Poetical Works*   2   (Chandos Poets: Warne, 1880)
CLASSICS
H. W. Dulcken (ed.), *Dalziels' Illustrated Arabian Nights Entertainments*   96   (Ward, Lock & Tyler, 1863–5). 2 vols
Cervantes, *The Adventures of Don Quixote de la Mancha*   100   (Warne, 1866)
W. R. S. Ralston (ed.), *Krilof and His Fables*   24   (Strahan, 1869). Also, London & New York edition: Cassell, 1883
ADVENTURE
W. Collins, *After Dark*   4   (Smith & Elder, 1862)
Ann Bowman, *The Boy Pilgrims*   8   (Warne, 1866)
Sarah Tytler [pseud. for Henrietta Keddie], *Citoyenne Jaqueline*   2   (Strahan, 1866). The one-volume edition only

NOVEL

Charles Dickens, *Hard Times* 1 (Chapman, 1866)

RELIGIOUS WORKS

J. Foxe, *The Book of Martyrs*. Revised by the Rev. Bramley-Moore 7 (London & New York: Cassell, Petter and Galpin, 1867-9). First published as part-work. Reprinted 1877-9

The Dalziel Bible Gallery 2 (Routledge, 1881). Reprinted with additional illustrations as *Art Pictures from the Old Testament* (Society for Promoting Christian Knowledge, 1894)

NURSERY RHYMES AND CHILDREN'S STORIES

J. Ingelow, *Stories Told to a Child* 2 (Strahan, 1865)

R. and C. Temple, *The Temple Anecdotes* 5 (Routledge, 1865). 2 vols. Originally a monthly part-work. Vol. I republished as *Invention & Discovery* (London, 1870); Vol. II as *Enterprise & Adventure* (London, 1870)

G. F. Townsend (ed.), *The Arabian Nights* 8. An expurgated edition not to be confused with the Dalziel edition: new designs

H. W. Dulcken, *Old Friends & New Friends* 2 (Warne, 1867)

Anon (Jean Ingelow), *Studies for Stories* 1 (Strahan, 1866)

J. W. Elliott (comp.), *Our National Nursery Rhymes* 2 (Novello, 1870)

SCHOOL STORIES

E. Eiloart, *Ernie the Lazy Boy* 4 (Routledge, 1865)

Ernie at School 4 (Routledge, 1866)

Patient Henry 4 (Routledge, 1865)

The Boys of Beechwood 8 (Routledge, 1868)

H. C. Adams, *Balderscourt* 7 (Routledge, 1866)

Barford Bridge 8 (Routledge, 1868)

Every Boy's Annual 8 (Routledge, 1866)

C. Camden, *The Boys of Axleford* 1 (Strahan, 1869)

MISCELLANEOUS

A. B. Thompson, *The Victorian History of England* 1 (Routledge, 1864)

A. Haliday (ed.), *The Savage Club Papers* 1 (Tinsley, 1868)

WEEKLY MAGAZINES AND NEWSPAPERS

The Welcome Guest 2 1861

Once A Week 12 1866-7

Illustrated London News 2 1865, 1866

Fun 22 1866-7

Graphic 105 1869-73; 1875

Every Saturday (Boston) 23 1870-1

Harper's Weekly (New York) 8 1870-3

Select Bibliography

BOOKS

W. H. DIXON, *New America* (London & Philadelphia, 1867). 2 vols.
Houghton largely based the itinerary of his American travels on Dixon's.

J. LEIGHTON, *Paris Under the Commune* (London, 1871).

M. JACKSON, *The Pictorial Press* (London, 1885).

P. LISSAGARZY, *History of the Commune* (London, 1886).

J. L. ROGET, *History of the Old Water Colour Society* (London, 1891).

H. S. MARKS, *Pen and Pencil Sketches* (London, 1894). 2 vols.

J. PENNELL, *Modern Illustration* (London, 1895).

L. HOUSMAN, *Arthur Boyd Houghton* (London, 1896).

F. M. HUEFFER, *Ford Madox Brown* (London, 1896).

G. WHITE, *English Illustrations: The Sixties 1855-70* (London, 1897; Bath, 1970).

P. BATE, *The English Pre-Raphaelite Painters: Their Associates and Successors* (London, 1899; rev. ed., 1901).

THE BROTHERS DALZIEL, *A Record of Work 1840-90* (London, 1901).

W. M. ROSSETTI, *The Rossetti Papers 1862-70* (London, 1901).

W. SIMPSON, *Autobiography* (London, 1903).

A. B. PAINE, *Thomas Nast* (London and New York, 1904).

HARRY FURNISS, *My Bohemian Days* (London, 1914). 2 vols.

F. REID, *Illustrators of the Sixties* (London, 1928; New York, 1975).
Chapter X, pp. 187-200, is devoted to the work of the artist.

R. V. MESSEL (Trs.), *Letters to an Artist. From Vincent Van Gogh to Anton Ridder Van Rappard 1881-85* (London, 1936).
Frequent references to Houghton and the illustrators of the *Graphic*.

S. SITWELL, *Narrative Pictures* (London, 1937).

H. REITLINGER, *From Hogarth to Keene* (London, 1938).

H. HARTLEY, *Eighty-Eight Not Out* (London, 1939).
The author formed the largest collection of the illustrators of the sixties (now at Boston). Chapter XXII deals with his interest in their work and his contact with the Dalziels etc.

G. BOURGIN (Ed.), *La Guerre de 1870-71 et La Commune* (Paris, 1939).
A well-documented history illustrated with photographs, cartoons and paintings, as well as sketches and drawings made by various Special Artists including Houghton, Simpson and Vierge.

F. D. KLINGENDER, *Art and the Industrial Revolution* (London, 1947; rev. ed., 1968).

O. DOUGHTY, *Dante Gabriel Rossetti: A Victorian Romantic* (London, 1949).

G. N. RAY, *The Illustrator and the Book in England from 1790 to 1914* (Morgan Library, New York, 1976).
Discusses Houghton pp. 176-8.

G. REYNOLDS, *Painters of the Victorian Scene* (London, 1953).

E. J. LEONARD and J. C. GOODMAN, *Buffalo Bill, King of the Old West* (New York, 1955).

H. TAINE, *Notes on England 1860-70* (London, 1957).

E. ROUTLEY, *English Religious Dissent* (Cambridge, 1960).

A. TEN EYCK GARDENER, *Winslow Homer* (New York, 1961).

E. D. ANDREWS, *The People Called Shakers* (New York, 1963).

W. E. FREDEMAN, *Pre-Raphaelitism: A Bibliocritical Study* (Cambridge, Mass., 1965).

E. THOMAS, *The Women Incendiaries* (New York, 1966; London, 1967).

G. REYNOLDS, *Victorian Painting* (London, 1967).

L. ORMOND, *George du Maurier* (London, 1967).

J. P. MAAS, *Victorian Painters* (London, 1969).

S. EDWARDS, *The Paris Commune* (London, 1971).

P. MUIR, *Victorian Illustrated Books* (London, 1971).

L. NOCHLIN, *Realism* (London & Baltimore, 1971).

K. CHESNEY, *The Victorian Underworld* (London, 1971).

P. HOGARTH, *Artists on Horseback: the Old West in Illustrated Journalism 1857-1900* (New York, 1972).
Chapter 3, 'Off to the Plains', discusses Houghton's travels in the American West.

E. P. THOMPSON and EILEEN YEO, *The Unknown Mayhew* (London, 1972).

R. MCLEAN, *Victorian Book Design & Colour Printing* (London, 1972).

E. DE MARÉ, *The London that Doré Saw* (London, 1973).

O. L. BETTMANN, *The Good Old Days – They Were Terrible!* (New York, 1974).

E. DE MARÉ, *The Victorian Woodblock Illustrators* (London, 1980).

ARTICLES AND CATALOGUES

W. L. THOMAS, 'The Making of the *Graphic*', *Universal Review*, I, September, 1888: pp. 82-6.

H. QUILTER, 'Some *Graphic* Artists: Arthur Boyd Houghton', *Universal Review*, I, September, 1888: p. 99.

Dictionary of National Biography 27, 1891: pp. 419-20.

L. HOUSMAN, 'A Forgotten Book-Illustrator', *Bibliographica*, I, 1895: pp. 275-90.

ANON [Gleeson White], *Forty Designs by A. Boyd Houghton*, 1896.
Catalogue of an exhibition at the Sign of the Dial, 53 Warwick Street, London, W.

J. PENNELL, '*Once A Week*: A Great Art Magazine', *Bibliographica*, III, 1897: pp. 60-82.

ANON [F. G. Stephens], review of Housman's *Arthur Boyd Houghton*, *Athenaeum*, 1897: p. 515.

H. HARTLEY, *English Graphic Art*, 1917.
    Catalogue of a loan exhibition of the Hartley Collection at the Royal Academy.

H. HARTLEY, *Book Illustrators of the Sixties*, 1917.
    Catalogue of the Hartley Collection, a loan exhibition, Tate Gallery, London.

E. J. SULLIVAN, 'Arthur Boyd Houghton – I: An Artist's Artist', *Print Collector's Quarterly*, X, 1923: pp. 94-122; II, X, 1923: pp. 125-48.

R. A. PARKER, 'Boyd Houghton's Graphic America', *The Arts* (New York), 4, I, July 1924: pp. 5-13.

G. DALZIEL, 'Wood-engraving in the Sixties', *Print Collector's Quarterly*, XV, 1928: pp. 81-4.

A. NEWLIN, 'Winslow Homer and Arthur Boyd Houghton', *Bulletin of the Metropolitan Museum of Art*, 31, 1936: pp. 56-9.
    A review of the centenary exhibition of the illustrations of Homer and Houghton (both of whom were born in the same year) held in the Print Room, Metropolitan Museum, New York.

P. GUEDALLA, *Victorian Life*, 1937.
    Catalogue of an exhibition of pictures of Victorian Life held at the Leicester Galleries, London.

S. HAMILTON, 'Arthur Boyd Houghton and his American Drawings', *Colophon*, June, 1939.

P. JAMES, *English Book Illustration Since 1800*, 1943.
    Catalogue of an exhibition organized by the Council for the Encouragement of Music and the Arts, London, 1943-4.

E. OWEN, 'The Golden Age of Illustration', *Sphere*, November 15, 1950: pp. 38-9, 51-6.

G. REYNOLDS, *The Victorian Scene*, 1956.
    Catalogue of the exhibition of paintings, drawings and lithographs held at the Leicester Galleries, London.

M. BENNETT, *Ford Madox Brown: 1821-93*, 1964.
    Catalogue of a loan exhibition organized by the Walker Art Gallery, Liverpool.

John Everett Millais: 1829-96, 1967.
    Catalogue of a loan exhibition organized by the Walker Art Gallery, Liverpool, and the Royal Academy of Arts, London.

William Holman Hunt: 1827-1910, 1969.
    Catalogue of a loan exhibition organized by the Walker Art Gallery, Liverpool.

A. R. LIFE, 'Leigh of Newman Street', *London House Magazine*, III, 7, 1972: pp. 36-40.

'That Unfortunate Young Man Morten', *Bulletin of the John Rylands University Library of Manchester*, 55, 2, Spring, 1973: pp. 369-402.

P. HOGARTH, *Arthur Boyd Houghton: 1836-75*, 1975.
    Catalogue of Centenary Exhibition, Victoria & Albert Museum, London, 1975-6. Includes checklists of Oil & Watercolour Paintings, Pencil Drawings, Studies and Sketches for Illustrations, Woodblock Drawings and Watercolour Drawings; and Published Illustrations. Introductory essay.

Index

Note: Numbers in *italics* refer to illustrations; see also Notes and Select Bibliography

Abbey, E. A., 78, *129*
'African Magician offers New Lamps for Old, The', *46*
After Dark, *41*
Allingham, William, *10*, 36
American Civil War, 61, 69, 70, 73, 85, 99, 101
And when did you last see your father? (Yeames), 35
Arabian Nights, 12, 43, 44, 47, 128, *129*
Argosy, *37*, *39*, 43, 123
Artist's Father with Cecily, The, *29*
Artists' Society, The, *see* 'Langham, The'
'artist with his wife and son, The', *26*
Art Journal, 21
Athenaeum, 17
Atlantic Monthly, 36

Baby, *24*
'Baden-Baden', 52, *53*
Ballad Stories of the Affections, 39
Barber's Saloon, New York, 66, *67*
Barricade in Paris, A, *115*, 117
Bartering with Indians, *95*
Bayliss, John, 127
'Bedmaker, McPhersons, Tuscola', *88*
Before the Bar, *126*
Benson, Eugene, 36
Bewick, Thomas, 36
Bickersteth, Edward Henry, *40*
Birmingham Society of Artists, 19
Bishop and the Gentile, The, *110*, 111
Bismarck, Otto von, 114
'Black Friday', 68
Bocquin, Lucie, 121
Bohemianism, 31, 32, 33, 35, 99, 119, 125
Borthwick, John David, 61
Boston, 80–5
Boston News Room, *80*
Boston Pets, *83*
Boston Police, *85*
Boston Snow Plough, A, 80, *82*, *83*
Boule Noire, La, *117–8*, 119
Boys of Beechwood, The (Eiloart), *38*
British Institution, 18, 19
Broadway Magazine, The, *34*, 35, 43
Broadway, New York, 66
Brown, Ford Madox, 11, 17, 18, 19, 35, 52

Brown, Major W. H., 101
'Buffalo Bill, King of the Border Men' (Buntline), 100
Buffalo Hunters, The (Sandoz), 100
buffalo hunting, 190, 103–5, 128
Buffalo-Hunting—A Jamboree, 107
Buntline, Ned, 100, 101
Burgess, John Bagnold, 123
Burne-Jones, Sir Edward, 36
Burton, Sir Richard, 111

California Gold Rush, 61
California Joe, 101
Callot, Jacques, 11, 41
Camping Out, 104, 105, *105*
Carrying the Mail, *98*
Cassell (publishers), 47
Cast of the Log, A, *62*
Catlin, George, 86
Caught in the Act, *14*
Chartist movement, 55, 107
'Childhood', *28*, 29
Choctaw Indians, 103
Christian Socialism, 19, 75
Church, Frederick, 85
Churchman's Family Magazine, 43
City of Brussels steamship, 62, 65
Coach and Horses, *26*, 27, *27*
Coasting at Omaha, 90, 91, 128
Cody, William F. ('Buffalo Bill'), 91, 100, 101, 105, 107
Collins, Wilkie, *41*, 57
colour, 128
Commune (of 1871), 113, 114, 117, 121, 128
Commune of Death, The, 119
Confederate, 55
Conjugal Difficulty, A, *20*
Conservative, 53, 55
Cooke, Nathaniel, 55
Cooper, James Fenimore, 85, 86, 92, 94, 99
Cornered, *111*
Cornhill, The, 43
Courbet, Gustave, 19
'Courtship', *21*
Courts-Martial at Versailles: Petroleuses Under Trial, The, *120–1*
Craig, Isa, *37*, 123
Crooked Hand, Chief, 97

Crossing a Canyon, *102*, 103
Crowe, Eyre, 61

Dalziel Brothers, the (Edward and George), 12, 25, *26*, *28*, *32*, 33, 36, 37, 43, 44, *45*, 47, 71, *122*, 123, 128
Dalziel, Gilbert, 35
Dalziel Fine Art Gift Books, 47
Dalziels' Arabian Nights, *129*
Degas, Edgar, 113
de Maré, Eric, 36, 55
Democrat (U.S.), 71
de Neuville, Alphonse, 113
Deserter, The, *16*
Detaille, Edouard, 113
Dickens, Charles, 33, 47, 49, 57, 111, 129
Dissenters, 33
Dmitrieff, Elizabeth, 119
Donkey Ride, The, *24*
Don Quixote, 47, *47*, 124
Don Quixote and Rozinante reposing under a Tree, *124*
Don's Discretion, The, *124*
Doré, Gustave, 47, 49, 62, 74, 113, 125
Doyle, Richard, *51*
'Dry point', 17
du Maurier, Emma, 33, 35
du Maurier, George, *8*, 33, 35, 41, *53*, 128
Dust Barrel Nuisance, The, 66

'Early Morning in Covent Garden', *56–7*
Edwards, Henry Sutherland, 55
Eiking, William, 127
Eiloart, Mrs Elizabeth, *38*
Embarkation, The, *60*
Emigrants, *64*
Emory, Brevet Lieutenant-Colonel Campbell Dallas, 101
Entertaining Things, *37*
Evans, Edmund, 36
Evans, Frederick, 75, 78
Evans, George Henry, 76
Every Boy's Magazine, 43

Family, The, *24*, 24
Fenians, 33
Fifth Avenue Hotel, New York, 65–6, 69
Fildes, Sir Luke, 49, 59

Final Procession, The, 78, *79*
First Buffalo, The, *103*
Fisk, Jim, 68
Fitzgerald, John Austen, 33
Flynn, Lord, 91, 97, 101
France, 113
Franco-Prussian War, 113
Fraser, Daniel, 75, 76
Friswell, James Hain, 51
Frith, William Powell, 15, 25, 57
Frog Town Runners, *84*, 85
Fun, 54

Gambetta, Leon, 113, 114
'Gambling Rooms, The', *51*
George, Henry, 76
Gere, John, 19
Germany, 113
Gladstone, William Ewart, 55
Gleyre, Charles, 14
Gogh, Theo van, 11, 129
Gogh, Vincent van, 11, 129
Golden Hours, 43
Goldsmith, Oliver, 15
Gone! (Holl), 57
Good Words, *26*, 27, *28*, *39*, *41*, 43, 71, 128
Good Words for the Young, 39, 43
Gould, Jay, 68
Goya, Francisco de, 11
Grant, General, 71
Grant, Sir Francis, 57
Graphic, The, 35, 43, 44, 49, 52, *53*, 55, 57, 59, 60, 61, 62, 64, 65, *65*, 66, *67*, 68, 69, 70, 72, 73, *74*, *76*, 77, 78, *79*, 80, 81, *82*, *83*, *84*, *85*, 87, *88*, 89, 90, 91, 92, 93, 95, 96, 97, *98*, 99, 101, *102*, *103*, 104, *105*, *106*, 107, *108–9*, *110–11*, 112, 113, *115*, *116–7*, 117, *118*, *120–1*, 123, *126*, 127, *127*, 128
'Graphic America', 52, 59, 62, 73, 111, 112, 123
Green, Charles, 57
Greenwall, Dora, *21*
Gregory, E. J. 57
Gronow, Captain Howell Rees, 23
Gronow, Thomas, 23
Gronow, Susan Elizabeth, (H's wife), *13*, *20*, *22*, *23*, *24*, 27, *29*, *32*, 33, 49, 51

Guthrie, Dr, *42*, 43

'Hairdresser's Window, The', 51
Haliday, Andrew, 37
Hard Times (Dickens), 47
Harper, Fletcher, 71
Harper's Weekly, 71, 73, 78
Harral, H., *115, 116–7*
'Helga and Hildebrand', *39*
Henley, Lionel Charles, 34, 35
Henley, Mrs L. C., 34
Herkomer, Sir Hubert von, 57
'Hiawatha' (Longfellow), *43*
Hiawatha and Minnehaha, 95
Hickok, Wild Bill, 100
Hiroshige, Ando, 41
historical themes, 15, 43, 124
'History of Prince Beder and Princess
    Giauhare, The', *129*
Hogarth, William, 11, 17, 41, 59
Hogarth Club, 18, 19
Holborn in 1861, 17, *18*, 19, 128
Holl, Frank, 57
Home Thoughts and Home Scenes, 47, *48*, 49
'Homeward Bound' (Allingham), *10*
Horsley, J. C., 15
Houghton, Arthur Boyd; family
    background, 11–12; early artistic ability,
    12; art education, 14–15; marriage, 23;
    family life, 24–9; early woodblock
    illustrations, 36–50; eye trouble and
    illness, 31, 32, 33, 34, 49, 128; in
    America, 61–113; in France, 113–19;
    final paintings, 123–8; death, 128
Houghton, Arthur Herbert, (H's son), 23,
    24, 27, 29
Houghton, Cecily, (H's daughter), 29, *31*,
    100
Houghton, Georgina, (H's daughter), 25,
    29
Houghton, Grace, (H's sister), 23
Houghton, Harriet, (H's sister), 127
Houghton, John Michael, (H's father), *10*,
    11, *12*, 23, 24, 33, 125
Houghton, Sophia Elizabeth, (née
    Renshaw), (H's mother), *10*, 11, *33*,
    126–7
Houghton, Susan Elizabeth, (née Gronow),
    (H's wife), *see* Gronow
Houghton, William, (H's brother), 12, 125
Houseless and Hungry (Fildes), 57
Housman, Laurence, 31, 129
Hughes, Arthur, 36
humour, 19, 31
Hunt, William Holman, 11, 18, 19, 36, 41,
    43, *43*, 125

Illustrated London News, 12, 53, 55, 61,
    112, 113

imperialism, 55, 112
'In Five Acts: V. The Fall of the Curtain'
    (Taylor), *33*
Ingelow, Jean, 40
Ingram, Charles, 55
Ingram, Herbert, 55
Ingram, William, 55
In Search of Buffalo, 101
Interior with Children Playing, *28*, 29
In the Rag Trade, 73
Islington Workhouse, 127
'It's a coming, and so it was', *38*

Jamboree, A, *106*
Jealous, George Samuel, 125
Jerrold, Blanchard, 74
Jewel Box, The, *31*
'John Baptist' (Bickersteth), *40*, 125
John the Baptist Rebuking Herod, 125
Johnson, Dr Samuel, 16, 33
*Journey of Prince Firouz Schah and the
    Princess of Bengal, The*, *44*, 46
Judson, E. Z. C., ('Ned Buntline'), 100
Judy, 19

Keene, Charles Samuel, 11, 14, 41
'King Beder transformed into a Bird', *129*
Kiss Me, *28*, 29
Klingender, F. D., 19
Kugler, Franz, 41

*Ladies Window at the New York Post
    Office*, 69
Lady with a Book, 22, 23
Lalla Rookh, 128
'Langham, The', 14, *14*, 15, 21, 31
Last of England, The (Brown), 19
Lee, Mother Ann, 75
Leech, John, *51*
Leigh, James Mathew, 14
Leigh's General Practical School of Art,
    14, 15, 31
Leighton, Frederic, Lord, 123, 124
Leloup, Marie, 119
Lemel, Nathalie, 119
Liberal, 53, 55, 111
Life at the Seaside (Frith), 25
'Life in A Year, A' (Greenwell), *21*
Life of Frederick the Great (Kugler), 41
Linton, William, 36
Liverpool Academy, 19
London (Doré), 62, 74
London Exhibition (1862), 41
London in 1865, *30*
London life scenes, *14*, 15–18, 19, 55–9
London Society, 43, 51, *51*, 52
Longfellow, Henry Wadsworth, *43*, 47, 85,
    86, 92, *94*, 95
Lytton, Edward Robert Bulwer, 15

Lost Child, The (Pinwell), 57

MacDonald, George, *38*
Mackay, Charles, 55
'Maid of the Woolpack, The' (Haliday), *37*
Manchester Royal Institution, 19
Manet, Edouard, 113
'Mansion House Hospitalities', *52*
Marchais, Josephine, 121
Marks, Henry Stacy, 14, 17, 23, 33, 35,
    123, 124
Marks, J. G., 15
Mathews, Charles, 14
Mayhew, Henry, 51
Mazzini, Giuseppe, 14, 35
McPherson, John, *91*
McPherson, Miss Betsa, *88*
Meacham, Joseph, 75
Measoms, W., *91*
Mending the Jack-in-the-Box, *29*, 29
Menzel, Adolf von, 11, 41
Meryon, Charles, 11
middle class, 11, 33, 55, 57
Midnight Sketches from Life, 127
Millais, Sir John Everett, 11, 18, 19, 36,
    41, 44, 52, 57, 123, 125
Minton Art Pottery Studio, 123
'Mock Burial, The', *49*
'More About Miss Bertha', 44, *44*
Morin, René, 114
*Mormon Family on their way to Salt Lake
    City*, 107
Mormons, 65, 107–11, 128
Morning Post, 55
Morris, William, 18, 35, 125
Morten, Thomas, 18, 34
Morten, Mrs T., 34
Moxon, Edward, 36
'Mrs Holmes Grey' (Rossetti), *34*, 35
Murger, Henry, 31, 32
Music Master, The (Allingham), 36
'My Treasure' ('R.M.'), *26*, 27

Nadar, (Felix Tournachon), 113
Napoleon III, 113
Nast, Thomas, 71, 86
News Room, Boston Athenaeum, 80
New York Herald, 71
New York Nursemaids, 66
New York Police, 68, 69
New York Veils, 70, *70*
Night Charges, 52, *58*, 59
North, John, 36
North American Indian Sports, 96, *96*

Off Queenstown, 65
'Old Gardener and Camaralzaman, The',
    45
On Board a River Steamer, *88*

Once a Week, 43, 55, 71
On the Scout, 105, *105*
orientalism, 12, 43, 123, 124, *124*, 128
'Other People's Windows', *50*, 51
Our Artist's Christmas Entertainment, 127
Our Mutual Friend (Dickens), 49
Out of Doors, 25
Oxford Street, London, 66
Oyster Stall, The, *19*

Pacific Railway, 61
Paine, Tom, 33
Palgrave, Francis, 123, 125
Papavoine, Eulalie, 121
Paris Commune (1793), 114
*Paris Under the Commune: Women's Club
    at the Boule Noire, Boulevard
    Rochechouart*, *116–7*
Parsons, Alfred, 112
Parsons, Charles, 71, 112
Pawnee Boys Playing Hoop and Pole, 96
Pawnees Gambling, 92
Pawnee Indians, 91–9
Pawnee Squaws, 93
Petroleuses Under Trial, 121
pictorial journalism, 43–4, 53, 71, 112
Pig-Driving in Cincinatti, 87
Pinwell, G. J., 35, 36, 44, 57, 125, 127, 128
Pioneers, 99
Playmates, *28*, 29
'Pleasures and Pains of Childhood, The', *48*
Poems (Ingelow), 40
Police Convoy in Boston, 80, *81*
Poor Nomads, 17
Portland Gallery, 17, 19, 21
Powell, Dr Frank, 101
Poynter, Sir Edward J., 123, 124
Pre-Raphaelites, 17, 18, 36, 41, 59, 123, 128
Prestcott, James, 75
Prinsep, Valentine Cameron (Val), 35
Proctor, Adelaide Ann, 27
Punch, 8, 53, 61
Punch and Judy, *16*, 17
Pyle, Howard, 129

Quakers, 75
Quilter, Harry, 35
Quiver, The, 43, *50*, 51

Rackham, Arthur, 129
Radical, 111, 125
Rag Collectors, 89
Raid on the Useless Mouths, The, 114
Rake's Progress, The (Hogarth), 59
Ramsgate Sands, 25, *25*
Reade, Charles, 57
'Ready for Supper', 52, *52*
Recruiting Party, 17
Reid, Mayne, 33

Religious Dance, The, 77
religious themes, 39, 43, 124–5
Republican (U.S.), 71
Republicans, 'Red', 33, 125
Retiffe, Elizabeth, 121
Return of Hiawatha, The, 94
Reynolds, Charley, 100, 101
Richardson, Joanna, 32
Roberts, C., *127*
Rochefort, Henri de, 113
Rossetti, Christina, 35
Rossetti, Dante Gabriel, 18, 23, 36, 37, 52, 123
Rossetti, William Michael, 18, 34, *34*, 35, 49
Round of Days, A, *10*, *21*, *33*
Routledge, Edmund, 33
Royal Academy, 18, 19, 34, 123
Royal Academy Schools, 14, 31
Ruskin, John, 19, 55, 75, 121

Salt Lake City, 107, 109
Sandoz, Mari, 100
Sandys, Frederick, 36, 125, 128
Saturday Review, 123, 125
Savage Club, 31, 33, 125, 127
Scallawag, A, 99
Scènes de la vie de Bohème (Murger), 31
Scene in the Prison at Chicago, 89
Scott, Sir Walter, 15
Scott, William Bell, 123
self portrait, *122*, *123*
Service in the Mormon Tabernacle, Salt Lake City, *108–9*, *109*
Shaker Evans at Home, *76*, *76*, *78*, 111
Shakers, 65, 74, 75–80, 111, 128
Shakers at Meeting: The Religious Dance, *76*, *77*
Shaker Sleighing Party, *78*
Shakespeare, William, 15, *15*

Sheik Hamil, *122*, *123*, *128*
Sheridan, General, 88
Sherman, General, 88
Shooting Turkeys in an American Forest, *91*
Siddal, Elizabeth, 23
Siege of Paris, 113–14
Simpson, William, 61, 113, 114, 117
Sioux Indians, 92, 103
'Sister Rose' (Collins), *41*
Sisters of Charity in Chicago, *89*
Slafter, Alonzo, *91*
Slafter, William, *91*
Small, William, 57
Smith, Joseph, 107
Smoke with Friendlies, A, *97*, *97*
social comment, 19, 51, *51*, 112
Socialist, 33
Society of Cogers, 31, 33
Society of Painters in Water Colours, 124
Some Reminiscences (Rossetti), 34
'Songs of Seven', *40*
Spectator, The, 17
Steerage Passengers, *64*, *64*
Stephens, Frederick George, 125
Stoke Hole, The, *62*, *63*
Stone, Marcus, 49
Storey, George Adolphus, 123
Strahan, Alexander, 39, 75, 123
Suetens, Eugenie, 121
Suez Canal, 61
Sullivan, E. J., 31, 34, 43, 44, 100, 129
Sunday Magazine, *38*, 39, *40*, 43, *43*, 44, 52, *53*, 71, 125
Swain, Joseph, 33, 36, 62, 90, 92

Taine, Hippolyte, 16
Taking a Nap, *91*
Taking the Waters at Baden-Baden, 128
Tammany Democratic Procession in New York, 71, *73*

Taproom of the Eyre Arms, The, *126*
Taylor, Tom, *33*
Tenniel, Sir John, 14, 44
Tennyson (Moxon), 36
Thackeray, W. M., 61
'*The Commune or Death'—Women of Montmartre*, *118*
Thiers, Adolphe, 113, 114
Third Class (Holl), 57
Thomas, Edith, 117
Thomas, William Luson, 33, 55, 59, 61, 71, 73, 113, 121
Thompson, Edward P., 125
Thornbury, Walter, 17
Times, The, 19, 107
Tinsley, William, 33
Tinsley's Magazine, 43
Toby Belch, Viola and Aguecheek, *15*
Tolstoy, Count Lev, 76
Tombs, The, *74*, *74*
Tourrier, Alfred Holst, 31, 125, 127
'To Whom it May Concern', *54*
Transformation of King Beder, The, 128, *129*
Trollope, Anthony, 57
'True or False' (Proctor), 27
Turgenev, Ivan, 35
Twain, Mark, 86
Tweed, Boss, 71
Twelfth Night (Shakespeare), *15*

Ukiyo-E, 41
Uncle John with the Young Folks, 12
Union des Femmes, 119
Unitarians, 33
United Family of Jones, The, 61
United Society of Believers in Christ's Second Appearing, 75
Universal Review, 35
upper class, 73
Utamaro, Kitagawa, 11, 41, 44

Ute Indians, 103

Victoria, Queen, 27
Victorian Underworld, The (Chesney), 16
Vie Parisienne, La, 32
Vinoy, General, 115, *115*
Vision of Sheik Hamil, The (Craig), *37*, *123*, 125
Vizetelly, Frank, 61
Volunteers, 17, *17*, 23
Volunteers Marching Out, 17, *17*

Wager, Thomas, 127
Wales, Prince of, 127
Walker, Frederick, 35, 36, 123, 124, 128
Wall Street, New York, 68
Ward, James, 15
Ward Lock and Tyler (publishers), 47
Warne, Frederick (publisher), 47
Watts, G. F., 57
Wentworth, F., *63*
Westmore, Helen Cody, 101
West Virginia, 86
Whig, 55
Whistler, James Abbott McNeill, 35, 125
White, Gleeson, 37
Whymper, Edward and J. W., 36
Wilson, Senator, 100
'Wisdom of Solomon, The', *42*
'Woman that was a Sinner, The' (MacDonald), *38*
Women Incendiaries, The (Thomas), 117
Women's Club at the Boule Noire, Boulevard Rochechouart, The, *119*
woodblock medium, 36, 37, 41, 43, 49
Work (Brown), 19
Wyeth, N. C., 129

Yeames, William Frederick, 35, 124
Young, Brigham, 107, 109